Along the tracks of Cobb and Co.

The Roaring Days !

History speaking for itself ...

Research and compilation by Hazel Johnson

In memory of the pioneers who built this great country of Australia

—through grit and graft.

Author's Note

"We should strive by might and main
To hold our precious prize,
To live in peace and harmony,
Beneath our sunny skies.
Think of those who have passed away,
They grubbed the great gum trees
They blazed the track with fire and axe,
All for you and me ...
Those were the times of grit and graft,
In the days of Cobb and Co."

Courtesy of John Elliott, writer/photographer

"We think of the stern austerity of the pioneering days retreating slowly before the onward march of civilisation, and we remember once again the ramping, roaring days when the Royal Mail was run by Cobb and Co. What a wealth of romance and adventure the very name suggests ... But oh ! they were good days ; rough days, quart pot days, damper days, perhaps ; but still they were big, brave generous days—days 'when the world was wide,' to quote Henry Lawson ... They were the days when 'There was work and enough for all hands to do, A snack and a shake-down for a traveller too' ... Here's to the old days—the good old days ; the ramping, roaring days of Cobb and Co." (The Day of Cobb and Co., 19 Dec 1908, p.12)

After five years of dedicated research, I have compiled a 'flood of recollections' capturing the roaring days of Cobb and Co.—a tapestry of amusing anecdotes, tales of grit and graft, and glimpses into the romance and poesy of the era. Staying true to my guiding principle of allowing history to speak for itself, each account preserves the language of its time. Authenticity has been maintained through faithful retention of original spelling, punctuation, and grammar. These elements, in themselves, enrich the narrative by tracing how language and thought have evolved over time.

I acknowledge that the accounts within this book series only briefly touch on the rich cultural heritage of Australia's First Peoples, and their interactions with others during the period of colonisation.

Note: 'Poesy' is an archaic term for the craft of poetry, dating back to the 14th century. It stems from the ancient Greek word poiesis, meaning "the act of creation or making," and remained in use to describe verse well into the early 20th century (Poetry Foundation, 2024). The phrase 'grit and graft' refers to hard work and determination—a hallmark of the pioneering spirit.

Acknowledgement of Country

We acknowledge the Traditional Custodians of the land
on which the Cobb and Co. stage coaches travelled.
We pay our respect to Elders past, present and emerging,
and extend our deep respect to all Aboriginal and Torres Strait Islander Peoples.

TITLES

Book 1
Along the tracks of Cobb and Co. —The Great Northern Road
(Tenterfield to Warwick)

Book 2
Along the tracks of Cobb and Co. —The Western Run
(Brisbane, Toowoomba, Roma & Charleville)

Book 3
Along the tracks of Cobb and Co. —The New South Wales Headquarters
(In & Around Bathurst)

Book 4
Along the tracks of Cobb and Co. —Back to the Beginning
(Victoria & the Goldfields)

Book 5
Along the tracks of Cobb and Co. —Cobb's Coach Drivers

Book 6
Along the tracks of Cobb and Co. —The Roaring Days !
(Amusing Anecdotes & Tales of Grit and Graft)
AVAILABLE AS AUDIOBOOK

Book 7
Along the tracks of Cobb and Co. —Queensland
(Brisbane & Beyond) (Release date … late 2025)

Print | Audiobooks | eBooks
Copyright by Hazel T. Johnson

First Edition February 2025, Reprinted July 2025

Content mainly courtesy of Trove (The National Library of Australia) and its many partners including State Library of Victoria, State Library of New South Wales, State Library of Queensland, State Library of Western Australia, and State Library of South Australia. Photographs taken before 1955 and maps created before 1955 are out of copyright (Australian Copyright Council). Spelling, punctuation and grammar as per historical sources. Every attempt has been made to ensure the correct use and acknowledgement of all sources. The information in this book is by no means exhaustive. Cover image: ca. 1884-1917 A Mail Coach Change (Kerry and Co., Sydney, Australia)—Courtesy Powerhouse Museum

Available from www.cobbandcotracks.au or local outlets

Further contact: email dvhtjohnson@gmail.com; Mobile phone +61 417984455

ISBN 978-0-6459759-9-4

This book was printed by: IngramSpark

Typeset in Garamond

Contents

4	Author's Note
9	**Part One: Anecdotes**
	—During the times of Cobb and Co.
10	Snake yarn No. 1
11	Another snake yarn
12	Cock-crow at daylight No. 2
13	The grit of the women No. 3
14	Quick thought saved them No. 4
15	Encircled by fire No. 5
16	Tobacco—people said it would kill us No. 6
17	Bail up ! No. 7
18	A stiff nip No. 8
19	Bushranger tricked No. 9
20	Blanketty-blank No. 10
21	Man forced to drink his horse's blood No. 11
22	No mail for you today, gentlemen No. 12
23	Startled lizard No. 13
24	It is an animal No. 14
25	Messenger of joy and sorrow No. 15
26	Shame ! No. 16
27	She's got another nipper No. 17
28	Before they have time to funk No. 18
29	Please explain No. 19
30	Mail dried in the oven No. 20
31	Mail bags on fire No. 21
32	Red as a lobster No. 22
33	Cabbage-tree Ned No. 23
34	The dignity of a box seat No. 24
35	The coach driver No. 25
36	A Jeremy Diddler No. 26
37	Electric shock No. 27
38	Flemington No. 28
39	Broken coach poles No. 29
40	Novel price-fixing No. 30
41	Lonely groom No. 31
42	A drowning accident No. 32
43	The fair sex No. 33
44	Christmas holiday No. 34
45	The last coach No. 35
46	You'll bah, you —! No. 36
48	Ashton Circus comes to Surat No. 37
49	Cobb and Co. No. 38
51	The coach's story No. 39
52	The Last Coach Southward No. 40
55	**Part Two: Poesy**
	—During the times of Cobb and Co.
57	The Dream of Gold—Alfred Pennyson. No. 1
58	The Roaring Days—Henry Lawson. No. 2
60	Eureka Stockade—William Jason Wye (Billy) No. 3
61	The Women of the West—Geo. Essex Evans. No. 4
62	Cobb & Co.—Marion Miller Knowles. No. 5
63	A Ballad for Cobb and Co.—Walter Robb. No. 6
64	The Rattle of the Coach—Will Carter. No. 7
65	The Coach Horse—Unohoo. No. 8
66	The Olden Days of Cobb & Co.—Wm. Jas. Wye. No. 9
67	Cobb and Co.—Will H. Ogilvie. No. 10
69	The Bushrangers.—Edward H. Morgan. Bowral No. 11
70	The Bushrangers' Cave—Ethel Mills. No. 12
71	Farewell to W. Rochester—Hawkeye. No. 13
72	Long Jim of Cobb & Co.—Bullman. No. 14
74	'Old Jack' of Coaching Days— Marion Miller Knowles. No. 15
76	The Whips of Cobb and Co.—Author Unknown. No. 16
78	To Mr Pat Gooley, of Messrs Cobb and Co.— J. Addison White. No. 17
79	Good-Bye to Cobb & Co.—Steve Hart. No. 18
80	The Ghosts of Cobb and Co.—Author Unknown. No. 19
81	Shadow Of Cobb & Co.—Hugh Stone. No. 20
82	The Last Coach—R.J.C. No. 21
83	The Lights of Cobb & Co.—Henry Lawson No. 22
84	Auld Lang Syne
86	The Days of Cobb and Co.—G. M. Smith. No. 23
87	The Days of Cobb & Co.—William Muggridge No. 24
88	In the Days of Cobb and Co.—Jack Moses No. 25
92	**Part Three: 100 years on**
	—Presentation by Hazel Johnson
101	Reference List - Images
104	Reference List

Part One

Anecdotes–
During the times of Cobb and Co.

1. Snake yarn

Let's get the wheels rolling with a 'snake in trousers' yarn ...

"According to a Northern contemporary (and these tropical papers hardly ever tell tarradiddles) man rushed into a pub on the banks of the Burdekin one day last week, yelling for help. Soon it was ascertained that a fair-sized black snake had crawled up inside one leg of his trousers. Willing hands helped the victim, and the reptile was, when extricated, found dead. As the man had felt many punctures, he was dosed with brandy for following two days, and then danger being past, tended like a prince for the rest of the week, at the end of which time he took up his swag and proceeded on his lonely tramp. A few days after the driver of Cobb's coach dropped in and, being told the tale, knocked the public into extravagant profanity by explaining that the man had played the same game at fully a dozen pubs and shanties along the road. The plan the gentle boozer adopted was to find a snake, kill it, and when in sight of a pub, lodge it in his trousers." (A Snake Yarn, 12 Sep 1891, p.10)

Another snake yarn

Toe chopped off ...

"Mrs. James Hammond ... who was looking after some pigs that were in the sty close to the house, felt something bite her toe, and looking down she discovered a large snake. She made all possible speed to the house, and got a young man that happened to be there at the time to chop off one of the small toes together with a portion of the outside of the left foot. Mrs Hammon displayed the greatest courage on the occasion, as she held her foot tightly grasped round the ankle on a block for the operation. The young man in the mean time, provided with a tomahawk and axe, laid the tomahawk along the outside of her foot from the small toe, and then struck it down with the axe.

> He had to repeat the blow four times before he took the piece clean off.

It seems the man was only recovering from the kick of a young horse received some ten minutes previously, so that after he gave the first stroke he became faint, and Mrs. Hammond had to tell him to go on and take the toe right off which he did after four blows. Mrs. Hammond is without doubt one of the stoutest-hearted women I ever beheld, as she endured all without a murmur. It is most wonderful to see the boot she had on at the time, as there is the mark of six of the snake's teeth right through the upper part, and the same six marks were in the toe, which was bleeding freely. She felt rather unwell all night and part of next day, but she is now, I am glad to say, doing as well as can be expected, and she is considered out of danger." (Adelaide, 1 Dec 1865, p.5)

"In 1887 the family doctor suggested ... many of our snakes are harmless and consequently a great deal of unnecessary alarm is caused ... The principal venomous snakes in Australia are the tiger, the black, and the brown or orange-bellied snake ... Thick clothing affords excellent protection by not only lessening the depth of the bite, but also by absorbing some of—indeed, sometimes the whole of—the poison ...

TREATMENT ... Professor Halford, to whom great credit is due for his researches, after numerous experiments came to the conclusion that the injection of strong ammonia ... would neutralise the poison. A series of experiments was made on dogs, but unfortunately the results were not entirely satisfactory. However, these attempts ... did much towards extending, the practice of administering drugs by injection into the tissues—or, as it is technically called, hypodermically." (Snake Bite, 13 Jan 1888, p.5)

During the era of Cobb and Co., snake bites—and the treatment thereof—were common and ever-present hazards! Now, returning to the story of Cobb and Co. (1854–1929): the firm began its operations with horse-drawn coaches in Victoria, soon expanding across the border into South Australia, and eventually reaching New South Wales, Queensland, and Western Australia.

Speaking of Queensland ...

2. Cock-crow at daylight

"It was one early morning in the month of November, 1875, before 'chuckle chuckle' as the term was applied in those days from the [First Nations people] interpretation of cock-crow, indicating approaching daylight, that I was aroused from my slumber at Joe Hodel's Hotel at Townsville by the sound of the mail coach bugle, and Tom Coyle, the driver pulled up in front calling out 'All aboard.' There were a number of passengers, with luggage, waiting to go by Cobb and Co.'s that morning. My mother, with baby in arms, occupied a seat on the box with two other ladies, and the inside was packed to its utmost capacity, including a younger brother and I, while two passengers were content to take seats on top of the coach, which was well stacked with mail and carpet bags. Portmanteaux and suit cases were not in vogue then—it was tin trunks, wooden boxes, or carpet bags. All the bulky boxes and trunks were packed in racks behind, and it took an expert at the game to pack then, and much rope was needed to hold them on, for no matter how carefully one packed them before the start, a word to the passengers on top to keep a look out for the dropping of anything was needed for the first ten miles stage. A change of horses was made at every ten miles, as far as I can remember (for I was only a lad of about ten years of age) and after the first stage it was customary for the driver to inspect and tighten up the slack of the ropes wound round the mails and luggage, caused by the jolting and bumping ; after that it was confidently considered it would be safer after its more settled firmness to increase the pace for the next stages. The coach was drawn by five horses, three abreast in the lead, and two in the pole, and the journey occupied two days. The old road was a round-about boomerang shaped road and was estimated at about 100 miles. Being so young at the time I found nothing to interest me in the journey up, consequently I committed nothing to memory beyond one little incident crossing the Burdekin.

Tom Coyle pulled up before going down the bank, and requested the inside passengers to stand up on the seats, as the stream of water which we were about to pass through would probably get into the body of the coach. There were three seats in the body, and twelve passengers occupied them, two ladies, six men and four children, and when they got to their feet on the seats and posed in a stooping position, all hanging on to one another, I can tell you it was a very awkward matter. I was compelled to take off my boots and sox and stand up between the doors and hang on to the sides as the coach proceeded. When we got almost through the stream the horses gave a bound.

> There was a splash and a loud crack of the whip, and the coach gave a sudden dip and a bump, and the water rushed into the coach up to the seats,

knocking me of my feet and a number of passengers sprawling on top of me. But we were soon out of it and it was a relief to comply with another request to get out of the coach after crossing the water, in order to lighten the load for the heavy pulling through the sand, and up the bank of the river, and thus get the benefit of a little exercise and allow the water to drip from my clothes before resuming my seat again in the coach, beside giving me time to subdue the sobbing from the fright and the wetting I got. All the other passengers were in a good humor, and seemed to enjoy the joke immensely. One old lady was very persistent in her queries of, *Did it hurt you, sonny? Never mind, we didn't mean it* for the rest of the journey in, and I was heartily glad when I heard the bugle call of the driver as we turned into Gill Street, below the hospital, on the way to the Post Office, to know that we were nearing our journey's end." (Memories, 14 Jul 1922, p.6) Other stories that demonstrate ...

3. THE GRIT OF THE WOMEN

The fabulous Mary Jinks ...

"Former Cobb & Co. coach driver Mrs. Mary C. Jinks, 78 ... says the girls of to-day lack pioneer spirit ... Girls of to-day are ruining themselves with smoking and gay life ... Her remedy: Bring back the Cobb and Co. coaches and give the young Australians a year on the run ... *I used to drive a coach from Broken Hill to White Cliffs opal fields (150 miles). I made the trip with a gun in one hand, the reins in the other. We had to watch the sundowners those days.*" (A Woman of the West Cracks her Whip, 22 Jul 1951, p.9) "Once [Mary] offered a sundowner a meal, but refused him rations as she had four young children. The sundowner, not daunted by the frail young woman, got rough. Mrs. Jinks was enraged. She . ran inside, found her husband's revolver, and with a bullet kicked up the dust near the sundowner's fast-retreating heels. But she does not think sundowners were such a bad lot. *Give them a feed even though they have no money and they will not forget you when they pass again—all cashed up.*" (Woman's Story of Hard Life on Mail Change, 25 Sep 1952, p.8) "For three years she ran the Mail Change at Kapala, along the route from Broken Hill to the Bunker Creek opal fields, and many a time she drove a change of horses out to replace a tired team and bring the coach in to the house. The drivers would blow their horns as soon as they were within hearing distance and, according to the tune, Mrs Jinks would know whether all was well or not." (She Drove for Cobb and Co., 22 Aug 1951, p.2)

And the pluck of Mrs. Empson ...

"A Croydon (Queensland) paper reports a ... Cobb's coach ... stopped near Rocky Creek and the driver and some of the passengers got down, leaving only a young man on the box seat in charge of the reins, and Mrs. Empson and a young lady inside. The horses took fright, and suddenly bolted down the road at full gallop. The young man on the box got frightened, and was quite powerless to check them. Mrs. Empson seeing this, with great pluck and at no small risk, managed to climb outside the coach on to the box, and when there seized the reins, and succeeded in pulling up the runaway team ... but the swingle bars broke, three leaders dashed off into the bush, and two of them were not recovered ; the third one was caught, and the remainder of the stage had to be accomplished with only three horses. Had it not been for Mrs. Empson's pluck and presence of mind there is no doubt that a very serious accident would have occurred." (Ball's Head, 26 Oct 1887, p.7) While ...

4. Quick Thought Saved Them

"Over a hundred years ago my great-grandmother, then a young girl, waited with her mother, brothers, and sister for Cobb's Coach to take them all from Queensland to N.S.W. When the coach arrived the coachman exclaimed: *Sorry! No room for bags.* My great-great-grandmother was frantic. What would happen to four young children, one a baby, in an Australian summer with no change of clothes? *Oh, what shall I do?* she cried. *Well,* said the coachman. *I promise to bring them down next time.* But my great-great-grandmother had been doing some hard thinking. *Will you wait awhile for us?* she asked. *Very well! But don't be long!* the fellow replied. She hustled the children inside and, quickly undressing them, redressed each, putting on two of everything, but making sure they had on the same outer garments as before. Those were the days of many petticoats, and you can imagine their discomfort. Soon they were all ready. The mother lifted each child into the coach, then climbed in herself. My great-grandmother at 89 still remembered the trip vividly. We couldn't move at all during that long, rough journey. Nothing did up and the heat and dust were terrific. But at last we arrived. Our ordeal was over and we had a change of clothes with us! The coachman kept his promise and brought the carpet bags on his next trip, but it was over a week later. It would have been impossible to manage without the extra clothes in the heat ... [from] Patricia Dearman (15)." (Contributions from members, 16 Apr 1947, p.10)

Speaking of coachmen, a "driver must be, and usually is, a man of firmness, activity and decision, with a most intimate knowledge of every road, rut, and stump on his line—his line being a distance of a day's drive, say about eighty miles, along which horses are changed as he travels backwards and forwards every twelve to fifteen miles, and the pace travelled at by the coaches is about 6 to 6½ miles an hour whilst going, or 5 miles an hour including stoppages to change horses, and for necessary meals to passengers." (A Bush Trip, 3 Jan 1880, p.18) For example ...

5. Encircled by Fire

"I rejoined Cobb & Co. as a driver on the Winton-Boulia run, a distance of 240 miles ... the trip took three days ... During this period I had many, happy times and many exciting (but some not so happy) experiences. My path was often blocked by fierce bushfires and I sometimes came face to face with their tragic consequences ... one occasion when being completely encircled by fire I decided to drive my coach into the Hamilton River. I let my horses go and walked two miles to the Hamilton Hotel ... The next morning it was impossible to go on, so we decided to ride out and see how the 4 men, who were fighting a fire ... were faring. The sight that met my eyes turned my stomach. Lying side by side with their hands covering their faces were the charred remains of three of the party. The other was lying alongside the buckboard. Stuck to the wheel of the buckboard as the charred flesh of this man's hand—evidence of the last attempt to reach water on the buckboard by grabbing hold of the red-hot wheel." (Death of Mr. S. C. Coleman, 16 Jan 1953, p.6) In that same year ...

6. Tobacco—people said it would kill us

"Australia, being the land of contrast that it is, gave me also my share of its floods. There were many rivers on the run, the largest of which was the Diamantina which crossed 52 miles from Winton. There were no bridges in those days. The river consists of 5 main channels and when in full flood was 3½ miles wide. It was during one such flood that I had my marathon swim ...

On this particular ocassion the river was at its peak and the boat was on the other side. There was no way of communication with Elderslie—telephone and wireless were unknown in that region. On reaching the river I saw the impossibility of crossing and settled down to wait—living for the first week on food supplied by boundary riders ... At the end of three weeks 40 people were gathered by that wide expanse of water. Food was short. Our diet consisted of mutton (without salt) and tea. Smokers had to satisfy themselves with a mixture of tea and gum leaves. The situation became serious and something had to be done. I volunteered to swim the river. I knew the country well, I knew the position of the channels and I knew where the shallow water would be. At six in the morning I stripped off my clothes and waded into the river. I made for what I thought to be shallow clay pans but to my exasperation found that they had been moved and that the constant attempts to find the bottom was taking too much out of me.

> I decided to swim from tree to tree, but found that the snakes
> had beaten me to most of these sancturies.

All day I swam then night came upon us. Dusk made my surrounding eerie and unnatural, and I was struck by the fear that I might lose my way. Then I spotted the evening star in the east and guided by it finally reached the other side at 9 p.m.—exhausted, my face raw from sand fly bites but with a great feeling of relief that I had succeeded in my arduous task and defeated the elements. I staggered eleven miles to Elderslie where I arrived at 3 a.m. I was given hot coffee and put to bed, where I remained for three days. The next morning provisions were ferried over to those on the other side." (Death of Mr. S. C. Coleman, 16 Jan 1953, p.6)

"These old coach drivers were hardy men. Summed up in the words of an old driver of 82 years, their elixir of life was plenty of fresh air. *Except on a few occasions, we were early to bed*, he explained, *and at 5.30 a.m. we were up, breakfasted, and ready to face another day of anything up to 60 miles. Pay was small in those days, and the staple meal of mutton and damper was so scarce that we never suffered from indigestion. We smoked vile black tobacco sometimes, though people said it would kill us, and had a drink occasionally. There was nothing better, though, than the fresh bush air and the scent of the old gum trees!*" (One Secret of Old Age, 28 May 1937, p.10) On the other hand, one of the perils of driving coaches was the threat of being stopped by bushrangers, sundowners, highwaymen, or "ruffians," as they were often known. These figures loomed large on the roads of the day, with countless reports of hold-ups and confrontations—some dramatic, others grimly routine.

7. Bail up!

"Mr. Richard Palmer ... 94 years of age ... was a driver for Cobb and Co. ... Once he was bailed up by bushrangers, and on another occasion he was present when a bushranger was shot dead by a constable ... While with Cobb and Co. he ran from Mount Victoria to Bathurst. Mr. Palmer later took over the run from Wallerawang to Cunningham Creek. It was in this service that his coach was stuck up by bushrangers. Mr. Palmer had pulled up to water the horses ; he had twelve women and two men aboard that day, and the usual mails. Captain Riley, who owned a station at Rylstone, was one of the male passengers, and the other was Mr. Bennett, Cobb and Co.'s manager at Wallerawang. The coach was being driven along quietly when two rough-looking fellows, named Stapleton and Rose,

jumped out of the bush and called out 'Bail up!'

at the same time covering the driver and those on the box seat with revolvers. A third member of the gang, McGrath, was holding his mates' horses in the bush. Mr. Bennett was driving the coach at the time and he was ordered to drive on and follow the leader—Stapleton—and the other bushranger into the bush ; Mr. Bennett hesitated, but Mr. Palmer, seeing the awkwardness of the position, took the reins and followed the bushrangers ; he did not want to be shot, he explained. The coach followed the highwaymen about half a mile into the bush, and the passengers were then searched, the leader at the same time threatening that he would blow out the brains of anyone who attempted to move. The women were searched first—some of them had tried to hide their money in the curtains of the coach, but it fell out, and the bushrangers seized it. *Whilst one robbed the passengers, the others had us covered with his revolver,* says Mr. Palmer. *As for me I never carried a pistol the whole time I was driving; it was no good trying that on, for if I had done so, and the bushrangers got wind of it, they would have shot me.* For that reason few drivers carried arms ... "

On that trip "Captain Riley, who had just sold some property, had a wallet containing some hundreds of pounds. This he managed to slip, under cover of his overcoat, into Mr. Palmer's hand, and it was saved. The mail bags were rifled, and the driver told to move off. *Later*, however, says Mr. Palmer, *I drove the coach back to the spot and recovered what was left of the mails. The bushrangers had hoped to obtain gold, but as it happened, they just missed a big haul by being a day late.*" (Early Days, 24 Jul 1931, p.7) In 1928, more reminiscing occurred as the coach drivers gathered ...

8. A STIFF NIP

"*A good coach-horse cost anything from £21 to £67 in those days*, said another old man regretfully; *you won't see such prices again for working horses*. Just then the chairman made an odd request to the gathering. *All those who were actually stuck up by bushrangers, please stand up*. But the old chaps were as full of fun as so many schoolboys, and every man Jack of them stood up. It turned out, however, that a couple of them had actually been 'stuck up.' *I was stuck up by Jack Morgan*, said Harry Watson; *that was in 1869, when I was driving the mail between Albury and Wagga. At Munga Park, it was, and*—But his voice was lost in a babel of 'I remembers.'

Were you ever stuck up? I asked of Bob Grover, of Wagga, aged 87. *Me? No*, said Bob, *but I've had some encounters with real bushrangers. In the Kelly days passengers and drivers alike were all keyed up and expecting the worst. I drove in the Kelly country, but I was never stuck up, because I always carried a bottle of brandy in the boot. More than once or twice I've swung round a bend to see Ned Kelly himself with his hand up to stop me. All he wanted was a stiff nip, and he always got it from me, and we'd swap a word or two. He was always alone. I fancy he was inclined to keep Dan, and Steve Hart and Joe Byrne in the background a bit. They were a bit too flash for Ned, I was in Jerilderie, New South Wales, when the Kellys stuck up the town and held it for three days. That would be early in 1879. There was a Government reward of £8000 offered for the gang after that, but no man, woman or child in the North-East squealed. They didn't dare. Only Aaron Sherritt, but the Kellys shot him dead at his own door. I remember*—his voice trailed off." (Those were the Days!, 8 May 1928, p.6)

9. BUSHRANGER TRICKED

During 1911 ... "A good story is told of the late Mr. James Dennis, one of Australia's best known hoteliers. In the days of the decaying industry of bushranging, ruffian entered the bar, and, 'covering' Mr. Dennis with his revolver, cried 'hands up!' *Surely*, said Mr. Dennis calmly, *it does not require two men to bail me up?* The bushranger who was on his own, turned round to see who was following, Mr. Dennis whipped out his own gun, and the game was up." (Bushranger Tricked, 9 Mar 1911, p.22)

Now surely there must be an anecdote about James Rutherford—hailed by 'The Founder of Cobb & Co.' (12 Dec 1924, p.4) as "the most enterprising man in Australian history." Rutherford was no ordinary proprietor; he steered Cobb and Co. through its mightiest decades with a vision that matched the open road itself.

10. Blanketty-blank

"A good story is told of old man Rutherford, who was for many years a member of the firm of Cobb & Co., the pioneers of coaching on a big scale in Australia ... Old Jim Rutherford ... the story goes that on one occasion he rode on to a wayside inn, tied his horse up to the lamp-post, and sat down to breakfast. He hadn't half finished, when in rushed a country man to tell him that his horse had broken away. He went on with his repast not deigning a reply. Five minutes afterwards another kind friend vouchsafed him the same information, but he went on browsing. When a third came along and told him about the breakaway, he ventured to look up and remark in a careless sort of fashion : *What's the blanky odds ? There's so many crimson people in this vermilion country who are always minding other blanky people's blanky business that they'll soon blanky well bring the blanketty-blank animal back.* And they did." (Personal Pars, 14 Apr 1905, p.8)

Next comes a chilling tale involving Cobb and Co. proprietor William Brown Bradley—a man whose name echoed across the coach lines, but who was no stranger to danger in the western country.

11. MAN FORCED TO DRINK HIS HORSE'S BLOOD

"The report I to-day send you will serve to show what a man may endure in these sterile regions. I have had many cases of hardship to record, but this of Mr W. B. Bradley, of the firm of Cobb and Co., is certainly the most fearful I have ever known. Men have wrestled with the terrible agony and died, but, since I have been on the river, no one has gone through as much and lived to relate the event ... Bradley says :—*About the 9th of April last, with a buggy and two horses, I started for back country belonging to us south of the Darling ... a distance of eighty miles without water. I had horses I depended on, but after going thirty miles through the bush one of them knocked up and I had to camp ... I had only two bottles of water, which were now consumed ... Having no compass ... I started next morning, one horse still very well, and went about seven miles when I believed myself too much to the east. I changed my course due south ... or what I supposed south, and travelled forty or fifty miles, and found myself among mountains ... which caused me to admit that I was in unknown country ; and had no water. The day had been very warm, and a painful sensation in the throat and tongue was felt; the horse was completely done ; here I camped. By daybreak I was after the horses, and found they had left me in the night ; found their tracks and with much toil (for I had eaten nothing since I started) ... followed them for ten miles ...*

About ten o'clock I came up to my best horse, the other nowhere to be seen ; and being in a fainting state from thirst, opened with my knife the neck vein, and drank more than a quart of my horse's blood. This horrible draught gave me much relief, but it was voided almost as soon as taken ... About 3 o'clock I found a kurrajong tree, and as well as I was able—for my knees trembled and my arms felt powerless—stripped away some of its bark, which I chewed, and found the sweet moisture of much benefit in clearing my throat and tongue ... and I felt convinced should anyone be in the like strait ... and have strength to procure plenty of this bark ... it would preserve life for a day or two. At 4 p.m. I again drank blood with exactly the same result ; my poor horse, Sydney, was now literally staggering ... All day it had been very hot, but at night it became quite cool, and I resolved to long-hobble my horse and follow him ... the reason of my hobbling him was that, weak as he was, he could out-walk me ... and even then I had to follow the sound of the chains. After going about six miles thus, he started into a reeling canter and stopped in a dry creek ... here I knew where I was ... ten miles had now to be got over, which took me about seven hours, when I reached one of my own tanks ... The horse, likewise found the tank, drank, rolled, and died ... the other horse got in the next day, and plunging headlong into the water, was drowned." (Terrible Suffering, 23 May 1868, p.11)

In fact Bradley, along with Rutherford and Whitney, became a partner in the firm of Cobb and Co. by 1862 when Robertson, Britton and Co. became Robertson, Wagner and Co. The same year Cobb and Co. expanded into New South Wales ...

12. No mail for you today, gentlemen

"Generally once a year, when the winter has been a wet one at the head of the Darling River and the snow commences to melt at the head of the Murray, there is trouble for the mail contractor running along these rivers. We had 500 miles of such tracks to contend with. The rivers overflow their banks, always by way of creeks or billabongs, and these are nearly always feeders of sometimes big lakes, being miles around, so that when the creek or billabong becomes too deep to cross, it means many miles extra going round it. Sometimes great risks are taken by drivers in crossing these places sooner than go around.

Each day the water gets a little deeper, and the horses get used to it, until you will see the leaders have to swim a few yards before getting their feet again. I've seen the horses swim and plunge twenty yards sometimes before they get their footing again, and the coach half floating and bumping. It used to be very risky work, and only horses used to it could get through. All mails, etc., and passengers had to be put above water line on top of the coach. I remember one incident in particular which occurred when crossing one at these creeks just below Salt Creek on the border of South Australia and New South Wales. This part of the Murray, I should think, would compare favorably with any other part of the world for snakes. They are there in thousands in the long buffalo sort of grass that covers the Murray flats there.

On this particular morning we stopped at one of these flooded creeks. Only the driver (Charlie Snell) and myself were aboard, and when the former surveyed the rise in water since he had previously, crossed, he remarked: *It's a bit risky today, but I think we can get across. Anyway, it will be the last time for a month or so. We'll have to go around the lake in future.* Just while we were making everything fast on the coach top, about a dozen snakes came out of the grass on to the road just in front and about the horses. Snell, a bit of a wag, looked at them, and said: *No mail for you to-day, gentlemen*, and turning to me, added: *I get a visit from this crowd every day. You will see some of them will escort us across the water.* And sure enough they did. As the horses walked into the water half a dozen of the snakes also, wriggled in, and swam across ahead of us, some turning back and others going right across. I remember that on this morning the horses swam and plunged quite thirty yards, hauling the five-passenger coach after them in the middle of the stream.

One of our old drivers, Andy Blake, was a wonderful man at getting along through these annual flooded conditions. My old friend, Mr. Fred Crews—now a retired, speculator living in Perth, but 50 years ago Adelaide's most dapper and probably best coach driver—used to be the mail contractor on this Murray mail for years, so I think he could bear me out in my remarks." (Coaching in the Commonwealth, 7 Jun 1925, p.11)

If the driver stories are to be believed, back in those days snakes were plentiful snakes ... Interestingly, it was in 1877 that "an antidote has been discovered [for snake bite] in Permanganate of Potash" (or Condy's Fluid) ... followed by "either by sucking the wound ... or by excising the part all round with a knife ... If the case is seen too late for the application of these remedies the best thing to do is to strive by all means to keep the patient alive until the poison is eliminated. Therefore keep him warm by applying hot bottles to his feet and give him stimulants. As in all these cases the breathing fails and death threatens by suffocation, special care must be paid to the performance of artificial respiration, a good method being to lay the patient on his back, with his head and shoulders slightly raised by a bolster, then standing at his head to take his arms just above the elbows and draw them well over his head (thus expanding the chest), then bringing them down and pressing them on each side against the chest (thus contracting the lungs), repeating the movement about fifteen times in a minute ... a very common and injurious practice, as is also the administering of excessive quantities of stimulants, the common plan being, in the country districts, to ply the patient with brandy." (The Family Doctor, 24 Dec 1877, p.3 & Snake Bite, 13 Jan 1888, p.5)

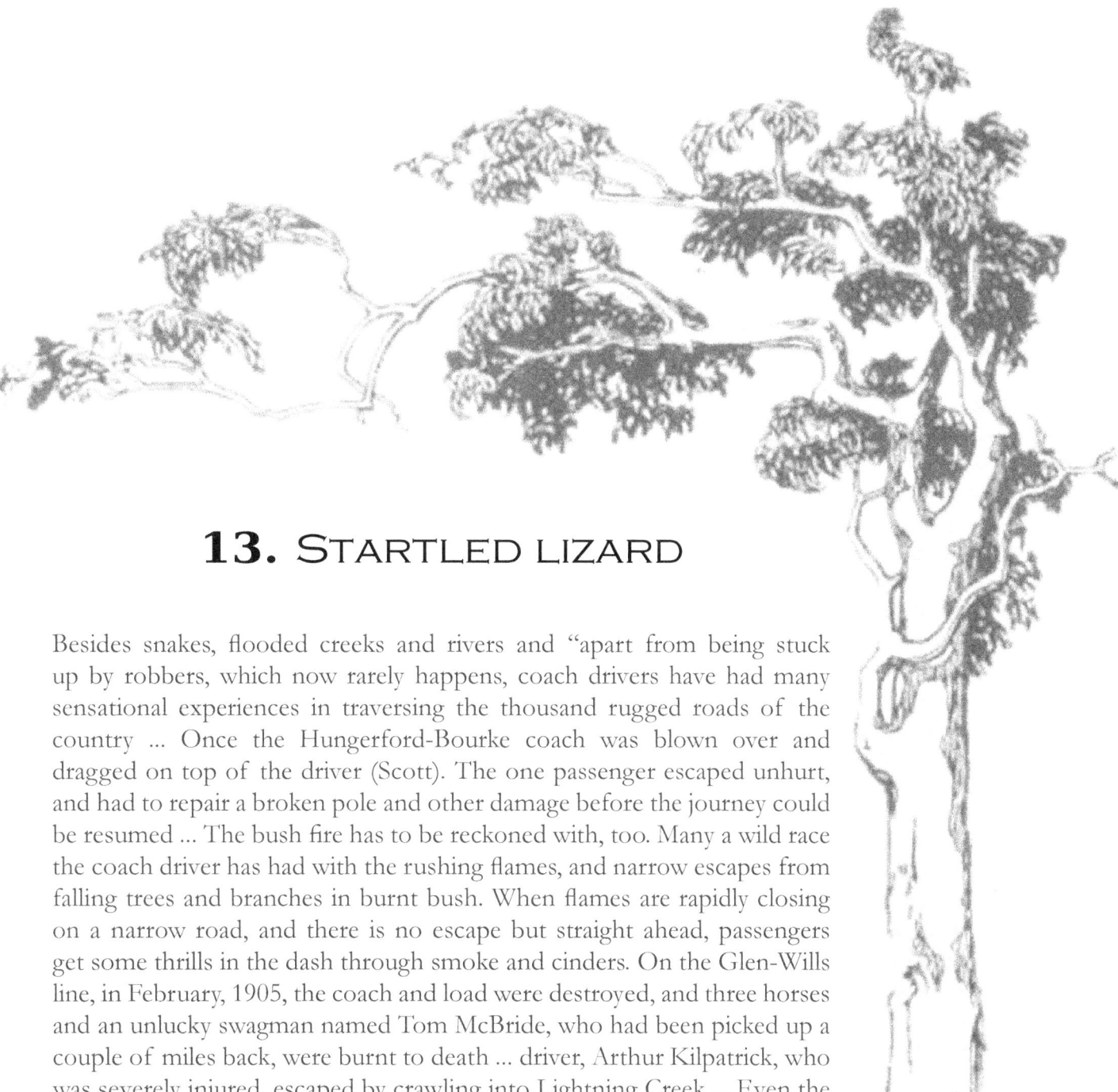

13. STARTLED LIZARD

Besides snakes, flooded creeks and rivers and "apart from being stuck up by robbers, which now rarely happens, coach drivers have had many sensational experiences in traversing the thousand rugged roads of the country ... Once the Hungerford-Bourke coach was blown over and dragged on top of the driver (Scott). The one passenger escaped unhurt, and had to repair a broken pole and other damage before the journey could be resumed ... The bush fire has to be reckoned with, too. Many a wild race the coach driver has had with the rushing flames, and narrow escapes from falling trees and branches in burnt bush. When flames are rapidly closing on a narrow road, and there is no escape but straight ahead, passengers get some thrills in the dash through smoke and cinders. On the Glen-Wills line, in February, 1905, the coach and load were destroyed, and three horses and an unlucky swagman named Tom McBride, who had been picked up a couple of miles back, were burnt to death ... driver, Arthur Kilpatrick, who was severely injured, escaped by crawling into Lightning Creek ... Even the common gohanna had a finger in the thrills. While the coach was travelling from Albury to Howlong (N.S.W.)

> a startled lizard ran up the legs of one of the
> horses, causing a bolt
> and a smash-up against a tree.

About the only thing, that escaped unhurt was the gohanna." (On the Roads with Cobb & Co., 4 Sep 1920, p.9) Speaking of animals ...

14. It is an animal

"A Cobb's coach is a 'Yankee nation' adapted for the rough roads of a new country—a thing of hickory wood, best steel, and much leather, exhibiting the greatest possible combination of lightness, springyness, and strength, with economy of space and carrying capacity. Ordinarily it carries six or nine passengers (jammed very tight) inside, and two on the box beside the driver. It is an animal (an animal being described as a thing of life and motion) with a large boot and an extensive tail, with a body between and a box in front, the boot and the tail being filled with mails and luggage. The body of the coach is swung on leather straps. Four horses are usually harnessed in front, under the guidance of coachy, who flourishes a long whip and keeps a firm foot on the break in descending inclines." (A Bush Trip, 3 Jan 1880, p.18)

15. Messenger of joy and sorrow

Now "every one who has travelled any distance in Australia is familiar with Cobb's Coach. In all the districts of the Colonies, to which railways have not been made, it is the common vehicle of intercourse. Freighted with people of every age, sex, and condition ; bearing the mails which set upon little communities like warm drops of life blood from the lungs upon the heart ; and almost ever on the move, it plays an important part in the social system of the Colonies. Eagerly is its arrival awaited at the isolated little township to which it carries news and influences from the busy populous coast town. Hopes are raised as the little cloud of dust marking its approach is seen far out on the plain ; and are gratified when welcome faces peep from the awning of its canvas cover, as the panting horses come to a stand at the hotel door. Many sad hearts look upon the bustle of its departure, and with tearful eyes follow it till it disappears in the hot glare of the noon-day sun.

> Messenger of joy and sorrow ; harbinger of good and evil ; bearer of the wicked and the just, the foolish and the wise, the strong, the weak, the wealthy and the poor—

though itself a thing of mouldy shreds and patches, of timber and iron and leather, Cobb's Coach a romantic, though very common institution. There are several varieties of Cobb's Coach—trim the rickety shandrydan, which carries three passengers and the driver, and travels weekly between very small brush townships, to the big accommodating type of stage coach ... that which set out from a little township in Central Queensland not so very long ago ... A square frame set on strong springs, contained seats for nine people. Six sat in the body of the vehicle—three with their faces to the horses, and three looking the other way over their companions' shoulders on the road passed over. Then there was room for two passengers on the dicky or knife-board, besides the driver. Mail bags were stowed below the driver's seat and the bulk of the luggage strapped on a light folding sparred shelf, that stuck out like a roasting brander from the rear part of the coach.

From the body rose a light frame of hickory, bent and fixed, so as to support a canopy of strong white oiled linen, that protected travellers from the strong heat and glare of the noon-day sun, and as occasion arose from tropical rain showers. Curtains descended from the canopy, which could be let down and fastened on by knobs, and then gave shelter from driving wind and the rain." (Original Tale, 18 Dec 1886, p.9)

Speaking of coaches ...

16. Shame !

"The other day, just prior to Cobb and Co.'s coach starting from Stanthorpe for Warwick, there was a man booked to go down by the half-past 12 o'clock coach. He was brought to Farley's Hotel in a spring cart, and was put in the coach and appeared to be in a dying state. One of the passengers objected to his going, and after slight demur, he was taken out and laid upon the ground in a very unfeeling manner, until some one cried out *shame*. He was then put in the cart in which he came and the only words he spoke were that that was a curious way of treating a man.

A doctor was sent for, and he prescribed brandy, but it was of no avail, the poor fellow was dead in five minutes.

No one seemed to know or care for him. His name turned out to be John Croaker." (Stanthorpe, 24 Aug 1872, p.2) While a good story about a nipper is recalled …

17. She's got another nipper

"Not so long ago since I was in a one-pub settlement consisting of ten tin humpies and 83 goats, and while having one with the publican, a tall, wrinkled cove drifted into the bar and ordered a rum. *And how's the missus, Dan?* asked the publican. *I hear she's got another nipper.* The rum disappeared, and Dan accepted my invitation to have another. *Oh yaas, she's had another*, he said in a far-away voice. *What is it this time?* asked the man behind the counter. *Oh, It's a boy*, replied Dan, *and that's nine we've got now. I reckon Billy Hughes ought to congratulate fellows like you, considering he reckons the country wants population*, I said. *Well, I'm doing me best*, drawled Dan. *You'd better have another.* As the publican picked up the empty glasses he remarked, *When was the youngster born, Dan?* The man beside me scratched his head for a minute and seemed to be burned deep in thought *I'm blowed if I know*, he said, slowly. *Let me see now. Yes Strawberry had a calf on Wednesday—a fine calf—a heifer, and on Thursday old Dolly had a foal, and the missus give birth to her nipper on Friday.* The publican smiled. *Really*, he said, *and what kind of a foal did Dolly have Dan?*" (On the Track, 31 Aug 1938)

And here follows another vivid anecdote—again featuring a plucky bushwoman and a resolute Cobb and Co. driver, each embodying the grit and spirited defiance that marked life on the road.

18. Before they have time to funk

"Good old Dick Palmer, who passed over the range last year at Cronulla, at the age of 94, once told me of many an exciting experience he had had during his long coaching service. One day, with one passenger aboard, and a lady at that, a driver found himself, during a stormy period of weather, confronting a raging flooded creek, just a little way out from Bathurst. He pulled up at the over-flowing bank, and stared pretty solidly at the roaring current, sweeping through a narrow channel. His passenger looked up anxiously at him and ventured: *What are you going to do, driver? Dashed if I know,* answered Dick, *it's ten to one we'll go down if we tackle that flood. Well, I simply must get over. I have a sick mother a few miles on who is without a single person near to help her in her trouble. If you are game to cross I shall not be afraid, and, perhaps I may be able to help you,* said the plucky bushwoman. *Well, you're a game one,* said Palmer, *I'll have a go for it, come what may. I'll go back a piece and put the horses at a gallop, and maybe we'll get over before they've time to funk.* Sure enough, they did get over, too, but it was a touch and go." (Australianities, 3 Sep 1932, p.2)

19. Please explain

"*Those were the good old days,* said Mr L. Sheraton ... *Wet or fine the mails had to get through,* he added. Western roads in the old days were not the best ... On his first trip it rained and as the coach chugged along the wheels collected heaps of black soil. At various stops the driver would have to 'debus'—to scrape the mud from the wheels ... *all western trips were similar during the wet weather,* said Mr Sheraton. Black soil roads had to be traversed and swollen rivers crossed. He recalled a man named Spencer who was groom for Cobb and Co. and camped at the Girley mail change. Spencer had plenty of pluck and he had no fear of flooded creeks. When the Diamantina was in flood Spencer used to swim the river with a rope in his mouth attached to which was a tub. First taking the mails across he would return for the passengers ... *And we were always on time,* he added. *They were strict in those days. If the mail was late there were 'please explain' forms to be filled in.*" (Reminiscences of Coaching Days, 23 Mar 1950, p.8)

Another mail anecdote written in 1878 ...

20. Mail dried in the oven

"The welcome forerunner of the regular rainy season with which we have been favored has not passed off without the usual disasters. A culvert on the Gympie-road, which, with the accustomed thoughtlessness of our Roads Department, had been left undistinguished by so much as a guide-post amid the raging flood that covered it, has proved fatal to poor Louis Bamberger, the faithful and obliging driver of Cobb's coach, which, together with the horses, toppled over the side and was lost sight of for hours ... On the coach, mail-bags, &c., being recovered, the greater part of the letters and papers were found to be saturated with water, and had to be dried in an oven before being transmitted to their destination." (Maryborough, 28 Dec 1878, p.6)

21. MAIL BAGS ON FIRE

Then in 1919 ... "A few days ago, whilst Cobb and Co.'s mail coach was proceeding to Augathella, about 20 miles from Charleville, the driver observed the mail bags on fire. He hastened to overhaul the mails and discovered that one bag from Brisbane was totally destroyed and other bags partly burned. The coachman in charge of the mails was undoubtedly a factor in saving from total destruction the coach and all the mails. The side blinds were burnt, but the body of the coach was not much damaged. A postal inspector has made a special investigation and took possession of two tins containing a certain acid which it is alleged was responsible for the fire, and consigned from Brisbane. The postal authorities are investigating, but are very reticent to furnish information." (In the West, 29 Aug 1919, p.6)

Indeed "there was a something of dash about those fine old drivers, and their teams, and the delivery of the Royal Mail" (Cobb & Co.'s Oldest Driver, 13 Jun 1930, p. 3) ... as "neither boisterous elements, nor mud-bound roads, seemed to interfere with the regularity of the mails, which invariably came to hand with remarkable punctuality." (Old Times, 29 Sep 1937, p. 8)

22. Red as a lobster

In fact ... "Early morning starts were a feature of Cobb and Co's service; in winter time it would be dark. We carried our own waterbags. When the destination was reached everyone would be tired, sunburnt and as red as a lobster. *But in those good old days we had no rationing, there was plenty of beer, plenty of butter and there was no need to worry about petrol*, he added. Mr May related an incident which cost him 25/-. Not desiring to spend Christmas out in the Never Never, he decided to make his way home to Rockhampton. So he took a horse at Muttaburra and rode, to Longreach, a distance of 78 miles. Cobb and Co. charged him 25/- for the use of the horse. Asked if it was a fact that he had bought all the vaseline in Longreach after his ride, Mr May said it took considerable applications before his flesh was back to normal." (Reminiscences of Coaching Days, 23 Mar 1950, p.9)

23. Cabbage-tree Ned

"Any of the skilled drivers of the great coaching firm of Cobb and Co. were famous in their day—especially the days of the bushrangers and gold rushes, when the roads of adventure threw them so much into public notice ... Of the hundreds of Cobb and Co.'s drivers, none caught the popular fancy or stamped himself on the tracks of time like Cabbage-tree Ned. As a whip he was famous in the boom days of Ballarat, and to the end of the coaching days his star remained undimmed by any driver on any road. Yet Ned never did anything very wonderful that scores of others did not do, except that he drove a huge coach that carried 70 passengers, besides mails, luggage, and parcels. But Cabbage-tree Ned (officially Edward Devine) was a picturesque figure, who got his classic title from the fact that he always wore a good Australian cabbage-tree hat. Ned was a Tasmanian, a dare-devil with the reins, who rattled down hills and swung round bends at a pace that made nervous passengers grip their seats and hold their breaths. It was said that when he was in a hurry, or had to make up time, some of the passengers shut their eyes in panicky anticipation of the crash of doom." (Whips of Cobb and Co., 24 Feb 1932, p.15)

Nevertheless, there was keen competition for the prized 'box-seat' next to the driver ...

24. THE DIGNITY OF A BOX SEAT

"The palmy days of Cobb's coaches, these were the days that made the name of the line a household word throughout the length and breadth of many lands, these were the days that immortalised 'Cobb', the good rough and tumble old times when it was a favor to get a place at all in Cobb's coaches, and the highest honor mortal men could aspire to, was to obtain a seat on 'Cobb's Box' … I have travelled many a mile with Cobb, always when I could, on Cobb's box. What special charm there is in a box-seat, I can hardly tell. It is certainly not the most comfortable position in the coach, exposed as it is to the broiling heat and choking dust of summer, and the piercing wind, rain and sleet of winter. And yet it has a charm, for who would brook to ride inside when by fair means or by foul, by force or by guile, by pre-emptive right or by open or covert bribery, he could beg, borrow or steal the dignity of a box seat? Not I, for one … An inside passenger … jolted and jarred … How different for him who shares the throne of the monarch of the road … He interchanges tobacco and drinks with the great man, he sits on the same seat, his legs are covered with the same rug. What more would you have?" (Cobb's Box, 6 Feb 1875, p.4)

Note: "Drivers of Coaches are hereby notified to the following Rule:—No ladies were allowed on the Box Seat of the Coach… A fine of forty shillings will be charged the Driver for breaking this Rule. Robertson, Wagner & Co." (Coach Poster, 1938)

25. The coach driver

"The wheel tracks of the Royal Mail are deep-rutted through the annals of the Australian bush, and the pilot thereof is niched forever in the corridors of Fame. He has followed the long, long roads to the outposts since the far-away days when the lights of Cobb and Co. first flashed along the highways to romantic, golden towns; one of the heroes of the hinterlands beloved of the poet, and who drives into a thousand stories.

> But though his team comes so much into the realms of poesy and romance he sees nothing poetic or romantic in it.

Jogging up and down the same old road every week, fifty-two times a year, for years and years, to him the ways are measured by days of toil and nights of weariness. He is a patient and enduring soul. One can realise this when watching him urging his reeking team over the great wide grey plains, and over the sand and stony hills, out at the back o' Bourke, when the little bulb in the glass is climbing up to the apex of its ambition. In normal, seasons his life is not one of ease and leisure. When the roads are sticky and boggy, and the coach is swaying and groaning under its heavy load, his best efforts have to be put forth, sometimes for thirty-six hours on end, to battle through on the long stages. On far-back roads there are few bridges and culverts, and a small flood renders many crossings difficult, at times dangerous, for washaways occur where least expected; and in big floods the water spreads over miles of country, so that he may drive for half a day without lifting a wheel from the wet. When the deluge catches him on the wide plains, it is not a mere matter of plunging through; it is a situation that demands resourcefulness.

But the long dry period affects him worse than anything. Over the wind-swept barren roads, through heat and duststorms, and all through the night, following a narrow winding track through the trees, across gullies and ridges, or over a wide expanse where a searchlight is required to distinguish the track from the rest of the plain, it is no joy ride to the man who holds the reins. But, wet or dry, the mails go through, and about the usual time the little crowd that gathers at the depot hears the whip crack down the road." (The Coach Driver, 26 Jun 1919, p.13) Now for a ...

26. A Jeremy Diddler

"Within the last few weeks, Goulburn has been honoured by a visit from a gentleman of the name of Edward Francis Clarke, who gave himself out as a nephew of Mr. William Clarke, of the well-known firm of William Clarke and Sons, gold brokers, Melbourne. Mr. Clarke took up his quarters at the Commercial Hotel, and stayed there for several weeks. On Saturday last, however, he announced his intention to leave for Sydney, and asked for his account, which was handed to him accordingly to the tune of about £21. Not having any loose chance, some of which he said he might require, he paid the bill with a cheque on the Bank of New South Wales for £25, and received about £4 in change. Having settled this matter to the satisfaction of himself and his landlord, he proceeded to Cobb and Co.'s office to book his place to Sydney. The fare £3, he paid by another cheque on the Bank of New South Wales, Goulburn, for £6, receiving £3 in change from Mr. Robertson, the agent. On Sunday morning he left by the coach, deeply regretted by the numerous circle of acquaintances be had formed at the Commercial. Monday being the Anniversary Day, was a bank holiday, and of course the bank was closed. On its reopening on Tuesday, however, the cheques were duly presented, but were met, not with funds, but by the statement that the drawer had no account at the bank, nor ever had. The result was that both the landlord of the Commercial and Mr. Robertson, found that they had been thoroughly duped. Information was at once given to the police, and a warrant was immediately issues for Clarke's apprehension. We believe, however, that as yet he has not been taken into custody, although there is good reason to conclude that he has not succeeded in leaving the colony.—Goulburn Chronicle. January 31." (Moruya Regatta, 3 Feb 1863, p.2)

27. Electric shock

Here's another "FUNNY STORY ... suspicion arose ... [about a] jockey ... The suggestion was that he had an electric battery inside his jacket when he rode ... This is perhaps the first time in the history of racing in this State that anyone suggested that a rider used an electric battery when riding. There was, however, a case in Western Australia. One day a boy was riding in a race, and in pulling his horse up the animal fell and the boy was killed. When carried in to the hospital his jacket was removed, and a small electric battery was discovered. How this is employed may be pointed out. The battery is fastened to the waist, and a wire is run down the leg of the jockey and connected with his spur. Then there is another wire passed from the jockey's waist and along the arm to about the elbow. To this is attached a piece of elastic, and the latter has a loop at the end of it. The rider takes this loop into his hand, end as he strains on it the battery is set in motion and connects with the spur. Well, towards the end of the race, when the horse is running home from the distance, the jockey pricks his mount with his heel, and of course gives the horse an electric shock. This is supposed to be an aid to making the horse put in a fast run to wind up with ... Some little time ago an old Melbourne trainer gave it as his opinion that a battery had never been used in a race at Flemington." (A Funny Story, 8 Jun 1912, p.21)

Speaking of ...

28. Flemington

"In its heyday, Cobb and Co. was the largest single transport system in the world. Besides playing a vivid and vital part in the development of Australia. Cobb and Co. provided a striking display at the first Melbourne Cup. An unofficial Melbourne Cup had been run the year before, but the first Tuesday in November, 1861, saw fleets of special coaches running a crowd of 4000 people to Flemington. They were going to see not only the races, but also a display which Cobb and Co. had promised, of the handling of big coach teams." (The Days of Cobb and Co., 21 Jul 1951, p.12)

29. Broken coach poles

While ... "in 1902 (I think Victory won the Melbourne Cup) I started with Cobb and Co and came to know such fine men and drivers as Jack Hiller, Sammy Drood, Jack Leary, Pat Cummings, Tom Lakewood, Donald Brenyer, Charlie Brayshaw, Bill Lumley and others—All great men with the ribbons and who, I understand, the majority have passed on ... Drivers carried hemp clothes lines. No, they were not used to tie the loads on with, but there were times when a driver got to a mail change or a roadside pub and he would be knocked up and lie down and perhaps doze off to sleep. If he did not wake when he should, he would probably be an hour late arriving at Walgett. The old chap would rush out and say *You are late, what kept you? I will have to report the matter*. Prior to this the driver had bound up the coach pole with a clothes line and his excuse would be that the horses played up and broke the pole. The PM would see the bound up pole. However, the excuse became rather common and one day the driver was late with the same old yarn. The old chap looked at the pole and remarked *My word, it must cost Cobb and Co. a lot for broken coach poles*." (In the Days of Cobb and Co., 19 Jan 1951, p.2)

However, "the breaking of the coach pole by fractious horses" did actually occur, so said driver Smiley on one of his 2500 trips from Warrambool to Colac. (Veteran Coach and Coachman, 8 Jun 1935, p.24) While driver Pywell ... adopting the practice of most of the coach drivers—a rather questionable one—had the reins of the horses separate, and when nearing the Victoria Hotel one rein fell out of his hand. Having thus lost control of one horse Pywell made an effort to regain possession of the fallen rein by clambering along the coach pole to which the horses were attached ... The coachdriver vainly endeavored to steer the horses by the one line of rein he held in his hand, whilst he unsuccessfully tried to pick up the trailing rein, and the terrible rate the horses were travelling at prevented him returning to his seat in the front of the coach. When approaching the wharf the horses swerved to the west side of Moorabool street, and in their mad gallop brought the coach into violent contact with the telephone post close to the office of Messrs. Huddart, Parker and Co. The crash was a very forcible one, as whilst the horses cleared away with the pole, fore carriage and front wheels of the vehicle, the main body of the coach was sent flying high in the air, and it fell in front of the office of the shipping company seven yards away, and Pywell was thrown with great violence into the mud on the centre of the road, where he lay motionless ... The coach horses dashed into the side of Leverett's conveyance with fearful force, overturned the cab and threw Leverett on to the roadway, a portion of the cab pinning him to the ground. The runaways then pulled up suddenly and were at once caught; willing hands released the unfortunate cabman, who was severely injured about the thighs, and had to be removed to the hospital. Pywell was found unconscious and bleeding from a wound over the right eye, abrasions on the face, and cuts about the right arm. In that state the unlucky coach driver was taken in a lorry to the hospital ... Owing to the accident the Portarlington coach, which is usually riven by Pywell, was somewhat late in leaving Geelong, another driver having to be obtained." (A Street Runaway, 9 Sep 1893, p.3)

30. Novel price-fixing

Now for some, "the mention of coach fares revives the oft-told tale of prices current on the Bathurst-Sofala stage in the early days, and it will stand repetition for what it may be worth. The road right through was extremely bad, but it was when Wyagdon Hill was reached that the main difficulty was met with. In those days the ascent was not a winding, graded way like it is to-day, but straight, and mightily steep, as all the hill-tracks were at the beginning, when the modern Roads Board was unheard of. On one occasion, when the coach was loaded heavily, a passenger said to the driver, *How comes it that you have three classes of passengers and three prices ? We all seem to be crammed to suffocation. You'll pretty soon get to know all about it*, said the driver. When Wyagdon Hill was reached the team was hauled up, and the man who handled the ribbons called out: *First-class passengers will keep their seats; second-class passengers will get out and walk to the top of the hill; third-class will walk and push the coach.*" (Gold-Digging Days, 18 Jun 1937, p.8)

Let's not forget the grooms and the change stations—known variously as changing stations, changing stables or way stations. ... such as ...

31. Lonely groom

"At the age of 12, I began work with Cobb & Co. as a groom at Dunbar mail change. My job was to care for the coach horses, have them groomed and ready in the yard when the coach arrived and to change them with those in the coach. My wages were £5 10 0 per month and I had to find my own keep. I remained at this job for 6 months. This 6 months was the loneliest period of my life. I was alone at the 'change,' living in a tent, and at night I could hear the howling of the dingoes and curlews." (Death of Mr. S. C. Coleman, 16 Jan 1953, p.6)

32. A DROWNING ACCIDENT

"On Thursday last a man named Benjamin Henry Bjorsten, the groom in charge of Cobb & Co.'s stage at Shanty Creek, in the Evesham Greysteel paddock, was drowned. It appears that on the afternoon in question Bjorsten went over from his place to a camp across the creek, which was in charge of Mr. George Medill, overseer at Evesham. After staying there some time he set out on the return journey. The creek, as a result of the heavy rain, was a big swim. Mr. Medill rode in a short distance with him and then turned back. The horse Bjorsten was riding turned up stream and then down stream. Bjorsten jumped off and tried to catch the horse by the neck, but as the mane was cropped, he failed. He sang out for help, and then sank almost immediately. A man named Corbett, who was also present, jumped in and dived several times to try and save Bjorsten, but failed to reach him. Mr. Medill procured a rope and hooks, and after three hours dragging the body was found." (A Drowning Accident, 27 Nov 1900, p.9)

33. THE FAIR SEX

"At frequent intervals were the stage horses or changing stables. Here a groom in charge was always in readiness to yoke up a fresh team, in many cases partly-broken in horses, and away to the next change. Many were the tales, humorous and tragic, recounted of these old stage horses and their keepers. Most of the old stories were true, others, due to the imagination of the old jovial drivers, intent on keeping his passengers amused, were doubtful. Of these latter, the gem of the road from Hughenden to Cloncurry was that of the courteous stage keeper, renowned for his gallant treatment of the fair sex. On one of the day stages where night accommodation was not provided, he never failed to respond to strange requests. In the case referred to a woman passenger demanded a bath, an unknown luxury at that particular time of the year. There certainly did exist, an old bag-enclosed space with a pull rope shower (out of order). To this the woman was escorted. Previously the gallant had filled a bucket with water, and standing on a box, waited until the lady pulled the rope, then he decanted the contents of the bucket over her fair form. Unfortunately she had retreated to a corner, and the water did not reach her. She was startled by a voice overhead, *Say, miss, stand in the middle, I'm blowed If I can reach you over there*. The woman collapsed, as also did the gallant water dispenser. After persuading the lady to resume, he conducted operations with his eyes closed, with the remark, *We will still continue to make your stay very comfortable*. So when she was about to retire she was handed a couple of squares of calico, dubbed sheets, but which were the only tablecloths in the establishment. As morning dawned the woman was disturbed from a peaceful slumber with the request: *Say, miss, please hand out the sheets, as I want to lay the table for breakfast*.

On another stage the story was told of the bloke and the pickles. He was a young commercial traveller, not yet used to bush tucker. When his portion of goat was handed to him, he asked the waitress for pickles. The fair damsel walked to the kitchen door and in a loud voice passed on the request as follows: *Missus, there's a bloke in here must think it's Christmas; he wants PICKLES*." (The Day Before Yesterday, 18 Dec 1941, p.41) Speaking of Christmas ...

34. Christmas holiday

1897 "Christmas Holidays. These will soon be upon us and for the lucky ones who can get away from the dust and dirt of Norseman, but possibly cannot afford time to leave the colony, we strongly recommend a trip to Esperance. Cobb and Co. have lowered their fares, and at 'our port' there will be found bright skies, pleasant people, a charming sea-coast, with safe bathing and comfortable hostelries. The Grace Darling, Royal, and Esperance Hotels are all replete with every convenience. Frank Aston can fix up jolly little oyster suppers ... Various other wants can be well supplied by Messrs. Vincent, Parker, Daw, and Fort, and the Esperance Brewing Coy." (Christmas Holidays, 11 Dec 1897, p.3)

By 1924 ... "Mr. Bruce, Prime Minister, has decided to make Canberra a Christmas box of the last coach used in Australia by Cobb and Co. Ald Brooks, M.L.C., president of the Federal Capital League, has been advocating for some time that because of the historical association of Cobb's coaches with the early development of Australia, the last coach should be secured and placed in the National Museum at Canberra. The Prime Minister wired on Christmas Eve that he was agreeable to the proposal." (Local and General, 31 Dec 1924, p.4)

"They were fine coaches, and one reason, why they were popular was this : They were supplied with leather thoroughbrace springs, which made them adapt themselves comfortably to the ruggedness of the roads of the time. The motion was more of a ripple than a jerk ... " (Cobb & Co.'s Oldest Driver, 13 Jun 1930, p.3)

35. The last coach

However, "coming events cast their shadows before, and each year marks a change in the order of things. Time was when Cobb and Co's coaches, their genial drivers and magnificent teams, were known throughout Australia, but the old order has changed, and the firm during recent years has rapidly with-drawn from being the principal purveyors of His Majesty's mails, and the carrying of mails by motor is being generally adopted. Looking over the many years that Cobb and Co. have served this district recalls the long mail routes traversed weekly, a few of them being from Mungindi through St. George and Surat to Yeulba, from St. George to Cunnamulla, and from Mungindi to Bollon. It also brings recollection of many noted drivers, some of whom have passed to the Great Beyond, while others have cast aside the leather ribbons to follow another line in life. There are many who remember Jack Warner, Jimmy Davidson, Ted Manning, Billy Mitchell, Dave Teys, and two local boys in Tom Anderson and George Douglas, who drove their teams through drought and flood, often under the most adverse conditions, in a tight hearted manner, endearing themselves to the travelling public, for with a genial and skilful driver the long miles of travel quickly passed away. The coaching teams were keenly selected, and there were many fine specimens of four and six-in-hand combinations that brought forth admiration. Notably among these was a team of seven greys that held the pride of place on the St. George-Surat line for several years.

Considering nearly half a century of coach service and at times the rather precarious conditions of travelling, the service was almost free from accidents, only a few of a light nature occurring. The coaching days, however, had their occasional surprise packets, one of these being the unfortunate predicament of a woman who gave birth to a child before reaching Yeulba. She was the only passenger, and needless to say it was a very scared driver that drove a rather knocked up team post haste into Yeulba. The Cunnamulla bank robber was brought by Cobb and Co. through St. George to Yeulba railway station, and a few months afterward suffered the extreme penalty of the law for robbery under arms. On one occasion the driver of the coach from Cunnamulla arrived at the rocks crossing when there was a higher fresh in the river than he imagined. When about half way across the strong current washed the horses off their feet and over turned the coach, with the result that the two pole horses were drowned and the mail was not recovered for a couple of days afterward a considerable distance down stream. On another occasion a constable was taking a prisoner from St. George to Yeulba, but when within a few miles of that place the prisoner jumped from the coach and made a run for liberty. The constable called upon the runaway to stop, and fired on there being no compliance with the request. The shooting was only too true, as it was a dead man the trooper carried back and placed in the coach. On two occasions, with a few years between, the mail was robbed a few miles out from Yeulba, when the coach was travelling towards Surat and St. George. The custom then was for the coach to start at night, and it is supposed that when it was negotiating a rather steep hill the culprit in waiting made a run for it and jumped on behind the coach where the mail bags were carried.

> The straps were cut and the mail bags dropped to the ground, they afterwards being opened and plundered.

On neither occasion were the police able to arrest the offender, and the mystery still remains. Valé the old coaches that were the present day link with the old pioneering days in this district." (The Last Coach, 30 Aug 1924, p.3) Speaking of Yuleba and Surat …

36. You'll bah, you –!

The town, Yuleba, was once situated elsewhere on the Yulebar Creek and it may be one of the most misspelt towns ever. Confusion may have occurred as it appears Mr. Lang's run, in 1851, was called "Horsetrack Creek No. 2, or Yeulba". (Adjusted New Runs, 22 Mar 1851, p.433) While in 1858 there was a run, "Yuelba, No. 3"

- 1859 Yuleba Creek ... seemed to have lost the 'r' at the end of the word
- 1866 saw "58 lots for sale, in the town of Yuleba, each consisting of half-an-acre, at the upset price of £8 per acre" (Government Land Sales, 1 Feb 1866)
- 1867 the "Sovereign Hotel's ownership was transferred" in Yulebah ... with a 'h' at the end of the word. (Advertising, 2 Feb 1867, p.1)
- 1876 saw a trip on the Western Road where the passenger said "We reached Yulebah or Eulebah ... where we found the Roma coach already arrived." (Paul Pry's Trip on the Western Road, 12 Aug 1876, p.3)
- 1879 appears to be the most confusing year. In March, at the Cross Roads near the Yulebah Railway Line ... a licence ... was applied ... for the 'Bushman's Arms Hotel'. (Advertising, 15 Mar 1879, p.2)
- April showed "New Yuleba has been gazetted as an additional polling place for this electorate." (General Epitome, 12 Apr 1879, p.15)
- June the Western Railway sought tenders for the "erection of the Booking Office, Platform, Station Master's House, Tank Stand and Ashpit, at Yuleba." (Advertising, 17 Jun 1879, p.3 & Classified Advertising, 17 Jun 1879, p.1)
- July in New Yulebar some eight or ten town lots were sold ... the 'r' is back on the word
- August, at the crossing of the Western Railway, over Yuleba Creek, the town of Baltinglass, had 89 town lots for sale.

Baltinglass was a total name change but this lead to complaints of letters laying at the Brisbane Post-office, address unknown. (Original Correspondence, 14 Jul 1879, p.3) A local resident wanted to know *Is it New Yulebah, Baltinglass or What?* Another resident wrote to the Western Star saying various names have been given to this unfortunate town-ship ... *the postmaster appointed was appointed for Ulebar Creek ... next the town was gazetted as Baltinglass ... Public Works tenders are for Yuleba ... the fourth name by which this place is known is New Yulebah ... I have resided here for a number of years and ... is rather hard that I do not ... at the present moment ... know my own address!* (Original Correspondence, 7 Jul 1879, p.3)

The opening of Railway to Baltinglass (Yulebah), was to be in Oct 1879 with another paper printing not long after "the newest section of railway was formally opened to Yeulba on Monday last." (Advertising, 20 Oct 1879, p.4 & Our Brisbane Letter, 31 Oct 1879, p.7) This spelling was continued with Cobb & Co. running their coaches for the conveyance of passengers and parcels to and from Yeulba via Surat to St. George.

Confusion continued ... 59 years later, in 1938, it was reported "There seems to be some controversy as to the correct spelling of Yeulba ... as government maps use Y U L E B A." (The Queensland Place Names Committee, 5 Jul 1938, p.9) Evidence shows by 1939 "the spelling of Yeulba has during the past few months been altered to 'Y U L E B A' (which should have been the spelling in the first place, but a careless railway employee, in putting up the name at the station, arranged the metal letters to read 'Y E U L B A' and thus it remained for more than 40 years. However, this has now been altered, and the P.O. has also adopted the spelling 'Y U L E B A'." (Cobb and Co., 29 Jul 1939, p.45)

How did Yeulba get its name in the first place? 1935 "One story I heard ... is to the effect ... that on a certain Sunday afternoon some of the navvies then constructing the railway went for a swim in a waterhole. A goat, seizing the opportunity for a change of diet, chewed up, unnoticed, one of the pairs of dungarees that lined the bank. When the owner discovered his loss he immediately gave chase with the idea of wreaking vengeance, and the goat, as it got into its stride, began to 'bah' in alarm. *You'll 'bah' when I catch you!* roared the enraged pursuer, and thereafter the locality became known as "You'll bah." (Yeulba, 2 May 1935, p.2)

Alternatively, in 1939 "Perhaps you have heard the story of how the place got its name. In the very early days an Irishman settled there and went in for sheep. He also had a few goats to supply him with milk. One day while he was milking, a rather wild 'nanny,' a surveyor rode up and asked the selector the name of the place. With the bellowing of the goat the Irishman did not hear the stranger speak, neither did he observe his approach, and sinking his boot into the ribs of the goat, he said, *'You'll bah, you —!* And Yeulba it remained." (Cobb and Co., 29 Jul 1939, p.45) Whilst ...

37. Ashton Circus comes to Surat

In 1876 "the bridge ... over the Balonne, at Surat, has been commenced ; considerable delay is anticipated owing to the scarcity of feed for teams." (Surat, 8 Apr 1876, p.9) By 1878, "the Surat bridge is now open for traffic, and when rain comes no doubt will materially benefit the town ... the same article said Ashton's Circus performed there with "the clever riding of Master Ashton and his sisters, and the daring performance of Mr Ashton himself." (Surat, 2 Feb 1878, p.7) Then a newspaper in Surat printed in 1886 stated that "Mr. Robertson said they were virtually re-constructing the bridge at Surat—the one they were building was a new bridge in place of an old one." (Bungil Divisional Board, 8 Dec 1886, p.2) "A high level timber and iron bridge, 350ft long ... the piers will prove a novelty in Australian bridge building." (Summary for Europe, 24 Feb 1886, p.3)

While on the Balonne, "Mrs. Dickens, her two sons and daughter were ... proceeding to Brisbane from St. George ... After starting, the horses, which were fresh, were driven eight miles without accident, until a gate near the residence of Mr. Healy was reached. The driver, James Murphy, gave the reins to Charles Dickens, a boy of six years, descended from the box, opened the gate, mounted again, and drove the coach through. Having done so he again gave the boy the reins, and having closed the gate, spoke to Mrs. Dickens' second son, who was inside the coach, and who wished to be taken on the box ... while in the act of doing so the horses started. Murphy clutched at the reins, and did his utmost to stop them; but one of the leaders kicked him, breaking his thigh. The horses then ran down the bank of the Balonne River, passed under a leaning tree, which knocked the top off the coach, and ran the vehicle against a stump, the shock throwing Mrs. Dickens out of the vehicle, and disengaging the horses from it ... Mrs. Dickens was picked up insensible.

Both her eyes were blackened and she had a contusion on the forehead, and another on the side, which caused her great pain." (Action for Damages, 26 Jun 1880, p.3)

Yes, Cobb and Co.'s horse-coaching faced many dangers—but today's challenge is ensuring its legacy doesn't fade into the shadows. Cobb and Co. played a vital role in the development of modern Australia—a history that deserves to be shared and pioneers who deserve to be honored.

38. Cobb and Co.

"Tchk-tchk ! Git up ! Hold fast there, and down the range we go, Five hundred scattered camps will watch for Cobb and Co" — LAWSON ... Good old Cobb and Co., big, lumbering and shaky—Cobb and Co. with its big bull's-eye lamp and its leather springs—Cobb and Co. with its leather blinds and its spacious boot crammed full of luggage—Cobb and Co. now mouldering away in its own dust in some long forgotten shed, helped very materially to make this country what it is. There are people who still say that the days of Cobb and Co. were the good old days ;

> the ramping, roaring, the happy days, rough days, quart-pot
> and damper days, perhaps;

but they were golden days, and the days of men, not machines. Now the iron horse speeds from centre to centre, laden with the argosies of peace and progress; but the railway train flies on panting and glowing in the night like some fiery demon, scarcely noticing the little villages and old time towns ...

Cobb and Co., V.R. Royal Mail—box seat, fare sixpence per mile, driver awful liar, swears like a—well another driver—starts from ramshackle Royals at unearthly hours in the morning, passes various Miners' Rests and Squatters' Arms en route, and finishes up alongside another Royal Hotel to the accompanying plaudits of the assembled townsfolk, who receive you like a long-lost brother. Sometimes you enjoy the privilege of a box seat and a good ducking as well, if you are travelling in the rain ; and if you were extremely fortunate you may have had the distinguished privilege of being 'bailed up'—a circumstance that provided material for a good story for life, and is handed down from generation to generation as a valuable heir-loom not to be lightly dealt with, but enlarged and improved as time goes on.

But if Cobb and Co. had its discomforts they were fully compensated by many a pleasure. What is grander than an early morning ride behind four spanking nags fresh from the mail-change on the hill, the fresh, crisp breeze of an early Austral morning blowing on your face ? The ringing, swinging music of pattering hoofs, and the rattling jingle of harness sounds merry in our ears. The dry and thirsty earth has been refreshed by recent rains, evidence of which still remain in little turgid pools along the roadside before us is a glorious panorama of undulating hill and vale.

On, on ! rattle, jingle! trot, trot ! 'And down the hill we go.' ... The soft, warm tenderness of early morn pervades all nature ; in the east the sun is rising majestic above a bank of grey cloud. We are passing a selector's hut; a little cloud of smoke curls lazily from the broad slab chimney ; three or four barefooted children clamber upon the slip-rail to wave their hats at us ... On past ring-barked paddocks, where stand tall trees, grim, gaunt, and grey—great silent, sapless sentinels in attitudes grotesque and despondent ; then past paddocks with sheep and wild looking cattle, who stand undecided whether to run away or face us. More scrub, another slab home, some cultivated paddocks, a small enclosure dotted with grave stones—God's Acre—'where the dead men lie' ; a rambling street, marked here and there by old fashioned cottages—the township, and we are getting down before the 'Travellers' Rest' ; in a few minutes we are in a long, low room, designated 'Dining Room.'

There is a strong smell of burnt fat, and we take our share of Ram, Lamb, Sheep, or Mutton. Ah, yes ! They were good days—the days of Cobb and Co ... along the roads there still remain old and ruined 'Travellers' Rests' and 'Squatters' Arms' to remind us of the days that are gone ; at the rear of these old ruins, with their broken, rusty, and crooked lamp-posts and sign-boards, now hanging dejected and useless, are big tottering wrecks that once were barns and stables ; old slab structures that once accommodated coach-horses and sheltered commercials' buggies; but they have out-lived their usefulness.

In some there are the remains of old coaches, and at evening when the light is soft, when the hot sun has sunk behind the hills in the west, little children climb upon the box seat, and clamber inside and play at Cobb and Co. ; me-thinks, if the spirits of the past revisit the earth, there are ghostly drivers on the box seat driving spectral coach-horses. And the old 'Travellers' Rests' and 'Welcome Homes' and 'Macquarie Arms' are aglow with light and laughter, as the spirits of the long-ago arrive or depart—by Cobb and Co's Royal Mail ; but there remains a fragrant memory, to many a perennial source of pleasure—or sorrow?

> For joys, wax dim and woes deaden,
> We forget the sorrowful biers
> And the garlands glad that have fled in
> The merciful march of years.
>
> —Gordon Valé!"

(Cobb and Co., 10 Jan 1903, p.1)

39. THE COACH'S STORY

"Half-hidden in a tangle of tussock and bracken, and bent low to earth as if to hide in shame from curious eyes, it lay — the forlorn relic of what had once been the pride of the road—her Majesty's mail coach …

Two crazy and nearly spokeless wheels alone remained to save it from utter collapse. Shafts, splashboard, seats, windows, fittings, all had disappeared. With its arms folded on the rail of a rickety fence …

What times I have had on the open road; glorious nights when under a full moon the shining quartz track stretched ahead like a silver ribbon, and in the frosty air the sharp ring of eight pairs of shoes made the sparks fly. Drab nights, when thick fog laid a clammy hand on coach and passengers alike … Days of storm and flood, when my passengers, huddled together in my cosy interior, were startled by a sudden opening of the door …

I served this district faithfully, carrying its people to and fro with comfort and safety … That was before speed became the god that most travellers worship … My limbs were now sending forth ominous creaks and groans with the weight of years, and my once handsome coat was sadly the worse for wear.

One dreary evening the horses were taken out of the shafts for the last time, and I was dragged to this unused paddock among other worn-out servants of man …

> Here I am useless and forgotten; yet I had my day
> — a long one, too — but it has closed.

The whisper died away to silence." (The Coach's Story, 2 Jun 1934, p.4)

40. The Last Coach Southward

We were camping by a gully, where the creek bed meets the road.
And the mail coach night and morning rattled by us with its load.
Somewhere on towards the morning, when the air was cool and soft,
And the dawn winds rustled gently, through the treetops far aloft.
Then we heard the mailman's bugle, and the crash of wheels afar.
And the driver he was driving by the light of moon and stars.

"Letter here!" he gruffly hailed us, "and a parcel from the store!
It's the last coach going southward, and we'll come this way no more.
For the train will come to-morrow—it's the day that she is due ;
She is loading over yonder, and she'll come like blazes through ;
You will hear her snorting westward as she thunders down the rails."
And the hillsides will re-echo to the train that takes the mails."
"Bearing north—for ever northward ; shift the rail head further on ...
Is the battle-cry of Progress. But the coaching days are gone.
Yes, the driver's days are over, and we're moving off the line,
But we'll toast them over yonder—for the sake of auld lang syne.

Now, at night I 'waken dreaming, when the curlews cry around ;
For a moment it's the bugle of the mail coach northward bound.
And the ghastly vision flashes from that dreamland to the eye,
Of a long array of horses and of drivers passing by.
But no hoof beats break the stillness, and no crash of wheels or bars,
Where they cross the ridges northward by the light of moon and stars.
There's a lonely rider riding in the shadows of the trees.
And the flooded creeks are running to the mail bags at his knees ;
There are drivers—weary drivers—in the dust and in the dew.
There's a ring of smoke and bush fire, but the mailman passes through.

We will never know their, story, how they went and how they came,
For the coaching days are over and are only now a name.
But when toasts to "farther northward" have been drank along the rail,
Let us touch our cups in "silence to the men who ran the mail."
— B. C. McAlister.
(Verse, 7 Mar 1919, p.4)

Part Two

Poesy-

During the times of Cobb and Co.

"Marvellous Melbourne, the Queen City of the South ... The discovery of gold gave the colony a wonderful impetus at the time ... they sought for gold and found it ... which fanned the excitement to a frenzy ... Victoria was crowded with searchers for fortune ... Who would recognise the 'bush town' of only thirty or forty years ago? The streets were full of gum-tree stumps and deep ruts and the principal thoroughfare, Elizabeth Street, was for months a year a flooded quagmire, in which bullock drays are daily bogged, and on one occasion a waggon and sum of horses were absolutely swallowed up. Iron buildings and bark 'humpies' were seen and what is now the important municipality of South Melbourne was a field of tents known as Canvas Town. Melbourne is now one of the most beautiful capitals of the world." (The Palace Hotel, 1889, p.79)

1. THE DREAM OF GOLD—ALFRED PENNYSON.

THE SQUATTING ERA.

The varying year with thickening fleece,
Clothes and reclothes the squatter's flocks;
He shears them clean, or in the grease,
And down he boils the cumbrous ox.
But lazily the hours rolled on,
As slowly from the cutty curled
The soothing vapour of the weed,
That makes men half forget the world.
No other sign of life appears

For miles and miles across the runs;
The grazing poleys, stags, and steers,
Wide horns, and down horns, brindles, duns,
Here seek among the water-holes
The surface of their shineing hides,
Or scrape against the gum-tree boles,
The covers of their rounded sides.

Even in town the slow clerks crawl—
The languid city seems to sleep.
The merchants, bankers, one and all,
Can scarce employ the clerks they keep.
In Bourke-street, half the shops are shut;
The publicans forsake their signs.
In short the Melbourne folks have cut,
By thousands, to the Turon mines.

Here sits a merchant at his books,
His sad eyes from the ledger turn
The luckless landlord's mournful looks,
Betray the depth of his concern.
The shopmen, undisturbed—alone
Behind their lonely counters stand,
And rumours right and left have flown
Of ruin to Victoria's land.

Oh when if ever shall be found,
A nugget on Victorian soil,
And who can say aurif'rous ground
Will here repay the digger's toil.
Yet all things must as now remain
Until the fated gold appears,
Come then prospectors mad or sane
And cause at once the change of years.

THE DISCOVERY.

The gold was found—the charm was snapt;
There rose at once a sudden trade,
And bankers laughed, and merchants clapped
On cent, per cent., and fortunes made.
The golden find enriched them all;
And Miller wept for joy aloud.
A hubbub shook the Civic hall;
And shouts and cheering shook the crowd.

The panic ceased, the prices rose,
The tide that ebbed began to flow,
For swift the news to Sydney goes,
Of Ballarat and Bendigo.
And all along the northern road,
With picks and shovels, carts and drays,
Men after men, and load by load,
Prospective diggers fill the ways.

Here lawyers quit their briefs and pleas,
Or hopes of briefs—'tis all the same,
There doctors cast aside their fees,
All bent upon a single game,
Merchants and scholars, rogues and fools,
Old, young, strong, weak, halt, lame, sick, well,
Pour forth with swags and diggers tools,
To meet a fate that time shall tell.

L'ENVOI.

You shake your head, a passing doubt,
Your finer sense of right offends,
Although the gold-fields be found out;
Say whereto such discovery tends—
Evil or good—the self-same thought
A learned judge ere now perplexed;
And so we leave—we think we ought,
Without response this question vexed.

(Australian Doubles, 29 May 1856, p.6)

2. THE ROARING DAYS—HENRY LAWSON.

The night too quickly passes
We are growing old,
So let us fill out glasses
And toast the days of Gold ;
When fines of wondrous treasure
Set all the south ablaze,
And you and I were faithful mates
All through the roaring days !

Then stately ships came sailing
From every harbor's mouth,
And sought the land of promise
That beaconed in the South ;
Then southward streamed their steamers
And swelled their canvas full
To speed the wildest dreamers
E'er borne in vessel's hull.

Their shining eldorado,
Beneath the Southern skies,
Was day and night for ever
Before the eager eyes.
The brooding bush, awakened,
Was stirred in wild unrest,
And all the year a human stream
Went pouring to the West.
The rough bush road re-echoed
The bar-room's noisy din,
When troops of stalwart horsemen
Dismounted at the inn.
And oft the hearty greetings
And hearty clasp of hands
Would tell of sudden meetings
Of friends from other lands—
When puzzled long, the new chum
Would recognise at last,
Behind a bronze and bearded skin
A comrade of the past.

And when the cheery camp fire
Explored the bush with gleams,
The camping-grounds were crowded
With caravans of teams ;
Then home the jests were driven
And good old songs were sung,
And choruses were given
The strength of heart and lung.
Oh, they were lion-hearted
Who gave our country birth !
Oh, they were of the stoutest sons
From all the lands on earth !

Oft when the camps were dreaming,
And fires begin to pale,
Through rugged rangers gleaming
Would come the Royal Mail :
Behind six foaming horses
And lit by flashing lamps,
Old 'Cobb and Co.'s,' in royal state,
Went dashing past the camps.

Oh, who would paint a goldfield
And limn the picture right,
As we have often seen it
In early morning's light ;
The yellow mounds of mullock
With spots of red and white,
The scattered quartz that glistened
Like diamonds in the light—
The azure line of ridges,
The bush of darkest green,
The little homes of calico
That dotted all the scene.

I hear the fall of timber
From distant flats and fells,
The pealing of the anvils
As clear as little bells,
The rattle of the cradle,
The clack of windless boles,
The flutter of the crimson flags
Above the golden holes.

* * *

Ah, then hearts were bolder,
And if Dame fortune frowned
Our swags we'd lightly shoulder
And tramp to other ground.
But golden days are vanished
And altered is the scene ;
The diggings are deserted,
The camping-grounds are green ;
The flaunting flag of progress
Is in the West unfurled,
The mighty bush with iron rails
Is tethered to the world.

(The Roaring Days, 15 Sep 1900, p.7)

Grievances on the gold fields lead to "the Eureka Stockade, where, on the morning of the 3rd December, 1854, the insurgent diggers, in arms against the oppression of the Victorian Government of that day, were defeated by the Queen's troops and police, after a short but determined resistance." (Niven's guide book and souvenir of Ballarat : the garden city of Victoria, 1880-1889) "There were all sorts here ... the police ... were pretty rough on the diggers. There was too much chasing and chaining to logs ...   After the Eureka stockade things were made better for the diggers." (Castlemaine, 30 Sep 1893, p.32)

3. Eureka Stockade—William Jason Wye (Billy)

It stands a monument of stone,
Upon Eureka Hill;
To warn the tyrant and the drone,
That freedom marches still.
It bears the tidings to the world,
Though Lalor's mates are gone;
That 'neath the Southern Cross unfurled,
The spirit still lives on.

It was to them a sacred trust,
Those stalwart men of old;
Who fought against the laws unjust,
The Godless lust of gold.
They were of Christ's own rebel breed,
That God's own throne might grace;
The enemies of graft and greed,
The chosen of their race.
"EUREKA HILL" brave sacred mound,

Where flowers in beauty grow;
Where martyrs' hearts' blood dyed the ground,
That day of long ago.
Australia's sons shall gather there,
To bow their heads in pride;
And honored be to breathe the air,
Where Freedom's vanguard died.

(Eureka Stockade, 3 Apr 1941, p.1)

"Perhaps sufficient has been written to remind some of the pioneers of the varied experiences & stirring times of … years ago ; while the younger men and women of the next generation will perhaps dwell for a moment in admiration of what has been accomplished by, their fathers and mothers as pioneers—members of 'the legion that never was listed' whose heroic, lion-hearted labor and womanly sacrifice has made the forest blossom with bounteous crops and pastures, and added a new and fertile province to the State of Victoria." (The Pioneers, 28 Feb 1922, p.3)

4. THE WOMEN OF THE WEST—GEO. ESSEX EVANS.

They left the vine-wreathed cottage and the mansion on the hill,
The houses in the busy streets where life is never still.
The pleasures of the city, and the friends they cherished best;
For love they faced the wilderness—the Women of the West.

The roar, and rush, and fever of the city died away,
And the old-time joys and faces—they were gone for many a day ;
In their place the lurching coach-wheel, or the creaking bullock chains.
O'er the everlasting sameness of the never-ending plains.
In the slab-built, zinc-roofed homestead of some lately-taken run,
In the tent beside the bankment of a railway just begun,
In the huts on new selections—in the camps of man's unrest,
On the frontiers of the Nation, live the Women of the West.

The red sun robs their beauty, and, in weariness and pain,
The slow years steal the nameless grace that never comes again ;
And there are hours men cannot soothe, and words men cannot say—
The nearest woman's face may be a hundred miles away.
The wide Bush holds the secrets of their longings and desires,
When the white stars in reverence light their holy altar-fires,
And silence, like the touch of God, sinks deep into the breast—
Perchance He hears and understands the Women of the West.

For them no trumpet sounds the call, no poet plies his arts—
They only hear the beating of their gallant, loving hearts.
But they have sung with silent lives the song all songs above—
The holiness of sacrifice, the dignity of love.
Well have we held our fathers' creed. No call has passed us by.
We faced and fought the wilderness, we sent our sons to die.
And we have hearts to do and dare, and yet o'er all the rest
The hearts that made the Nation were the Women of the West.

(Original Poetry, 21 Sep 1901, p.50)

"When gold was discovered in Victoria, in 1851, and up to the middle of 1853, the only means of conveyance to the then existing gold fields, Mount Alexander, Bendigo, and Ballarat, was by paying a carrier so much for head for the carrying of the passengers' swags and tools, the men walking, and, of course, camping out at night. The average daily distance was 25 or 30 miles, and for this each man was charged £3, finding himself in food on the road." (The Contributor, 25 Nov 1908, p.1405) "The fare to Forest Creek [Mount Alexander] was £3, the journey, 75 miles, occupying two days, the passengers camping out one night en route. This style of conveyance continued until the beginning of 1853." (Reminiscences of Cobb and Co., 14 Jan 1898, p.2)

"About the middle of 1853 a change came over this mode of transit." (The Contributor, 25 Nov 1908, p.1405) In mid-1853 "Freeman Cobb came to Melbourne … with George Mowton, to form a branch of Adam and Co, famed in the United States as express carriers." (Death of the Founder of Cobb and Co., 28 Sep 1878, p.3) "About the end of 1853 was to be seen any day in Collins-street, at, and about Adams' Express Office, which stood then just about where the Bank of N.S.W. now stands, a small, thin, wiry little man, slightly lame … This was Freeman Cobb" (Reminiscences of Cobb and Co., 14 Jan 1898, p.2) "carrying from Liardet's (Port Melbourne) to the City of Melbourne for a start but 'no road' across the swamp between Emerald Hill, now South Melbourne, and the river was such a quagmire that their waggons sank to the hubs." (a [?] Drive, 31 July 1937, p.4) "Hauling their waggons through the mud … they gave it up." (Old Coaching Days, 10 Jun 1922, p.7) "They advised their principals in the United States [Adams and Co.] against the carrying business, but told them that there was a good opening for a real up-to-date line of coaches to the diggings … the United States companies turned down the coaching proposition." (a [?] Drive, 31 July 1937, p.4)

"George Francis Train … says: *I told Freeman Cobb, who was then with Adams and Co., that I wanted him to start a line of coaches between Melbourne and the gold-mines, a distance of about sixty miles. I advanced the money for the enterprise, and a line was established, the first in Australia.*" (My Life of Many States and Foreign Lands, 1902, pp.133-134) Hence the beginning of the "American Telegraph Line of Coaches.— Daily Communication between Melbourne, Forest Creek and Bendigo … The first coach will start from the Criterion, on Monday, January 30th, and every attention will be given to ensure punctuality Cobb and Co., Proprietors." (Advertising, 31 Jan 1854, p.3)

5. Cobb & Co.—Marion Miller Knowles.

Here's a song of Cobb and Co.,
And coaches 'rhythmic rattle.
Crack o' whip and lusty voice,
On the uphill battle.
Distant views and rounding turns—
Ever still ascending—
Lilt of birds and hillside streams.
With men's singing blended.

(Annual report/Cobb & Co.'s Old Coach Drivers' Association, 1942, pp.6&7)

6. A Ballad for Cobb and Co.–Walter Robb.

There's a name, that will live in our Austral lands,
Till the sun shall decline to glow
On the ranges and gullies and coral strands,
And the rivers that flood and flow ;
It awakens the fanciful visions fast
Of the glorious days in the vanish'd past,
And we find it in—'Cobb, and Co !'

'All aboard !' it was then, as they dashed away
From the Albion in great Bourke,
With their spirits agog with the yellow ray,
And some whiskey, or I'm a Turk.
And 'twas good-luck to many, and middling to more,
In the reign of the Cobb and the golden ore,
But the workers no work did shirk.

To the axle in ruts, and a heave o'er the stumps,
In the days that had few compeers ;
O'er the corduroy road, with its rollicking bumps,
And a cargo of pioneers.
Aye, the brave pioneers—rugged battlers of old,

Whose pulses were stirred with the dream of gold,
In the Cobb and Co. dashing years !
Ev'ry bosom expectantly flutter'd then
With a hope that was something new,
In a land that was fresh to the ways of men—
The ubiquitous white-skinn'd crew.
Yet the glamour and charm of the novel sight
Has vanish'd for ever, like yesternight,
And echoes repeat—'Adieu !'

There are many yet living to tell the tale
Of the swaggering coaching days,
When the nuggets flew round like a shower o hail,
And the fun of the bullock drays ;
Of the roar of the camps, and many a spree,
And the hardships that prefaced a digger's glee—.
When he struck on the patch that pay !

But, quick presto ! a change o'er the scene has set,
And the railway is all the go.
Yet the days of the coach we shall ne'er forget,
Nor a ballad for Cobb and Co. !
For they carried the men who unwrapt the land,
And whose legacy lives, and for aye shall stand
For their sons to admire and know.

(A Ballad for Cobb and Co., 15 May 1902, p.15)

"Cobb's three original partners … a very simple fact … were John Lamber, James Swanton, and John Murray Peck … within 12 months Lamber retired and Arthur Blake came into the partnership … The famous 'Jack' or 40 passenger and six-horse coaches brought to Australia … did so much to enhance and spread the fame of Cobb and Co. They were all thorough-brace swung, and turned out to be the most suitable and popular for the purposes of the goldfields traffic on the main roads … Thanks to the activities of the Central Road Board, conditions of travel were rapidly improving." (Old Coaching Days, 10 Jun 1922, p.7)

Note: A detailed account of the founders of Cobb and Co., along with an extensive overview of its proprietors, coaching routes and change stations can be found in other books in the 'Along the tracks of Cobb and Co.' Book Series.

7. THE RATTLE OF THE COACH—WILL CARTER.

Three times a week they listen
The bush folks far away
From city rush and rattle,
From all the busy battle,
Out where the sheep and cattle
Ever stray ;
On Monday, Wednesday, Friday,
Impatient they approach,
And listen at the corner
For the rattle of the coach.

And thrice a week within them
The Bushmen's hearts are glad
When, oft, in gloomy weather,
When 'Blues' of evil feather,
Might send them altogether
Raving mad,
They wait around the corner,
And see the World approach,
And bring the Bush its message,
With the rattle of the coach.

(The Rattle of the Coach, 26 Dec 1906, p. 1650)

8. THE COACH HORSE—UNOHOO.

Stanch to the collar, there he stood,
A horse of worn-out frame,
While all the gathering multitude
Were crowding just the same.
The scars his sides and haunches bore
Showed where the lash had been,
And cuts and wounds, all fresh and sore,
Were on his shoulders seen.
He tugged and pulled with all his might,
While sharp the whip-lash stung,
As hard he worked from morn to night,
Nor from the collar hung.
He looked up in his driver's face
With wild beseeching eye ;
But naught of mercy could he trace,
Nor gleam of hope descry.
Once more he tugged upon his way,
Though hard the metalled road,
And hot the scorching sun all day,
And wearisome the load.
Crazed was his brain, and wild his eye,
Beneath the blinding sun ;
He staggered, reeled, laid down to die,
And then his work was done.

(Poetry, Original and Selected, 22 Jan 1872)

9. The Olden Days of Cobb & Co.—Wm. Jas. Wye.

As wistfully we close our eyes,
We seem to see beyond the gates,
And on the box seat, visualize
The welcome from our old time mates,
They're beautiful, those spectre teams,
And as we near life's sunsets glow,
'Tis good to live again in dreams,
The olden days of Cobb & Co.

(1940-1941 Cobb & Co.'s Old Coach Drivers' Association)

"The coaches of this line [Cobb and Co.] spread from the Great centre like a network over the colony—going direct to Swan Hill, communicating with Deniliquin and Moama, and performing daily journeys to Melbourne, Ballarat, Ararat, and the intermediate places. Twenty-six coaches belonging to this firm arrive at and depart from Castlemaine daily ; and the horses they possess number over 600. To these great dimensions has Freeman Cobb's 'speculation' expanded in the course of a few years.—M. A. Mail." (Title Deeds, 16 Sep 1859, p.3)

By North and South, by East and West,
By dawn and dark and day,

10. COBB AND CO.—WILL H. OGILVIE.

By swamp and plain and mountain crest
They take the foremost way;
And where the slanting sun-rays dip
And underneath the stars
Is heard the thunder of the whip
And creaking of the bars;
And out beyond the reach of rail
As far as wheel-tracks go
The drovers round their camp-fire hail
The lights of Cobb and Co.

The settlers wait at death o' day
To hear their rolling wheels,
Where faintly through the twilight grey
The far whip challenge steals;
They take the messages of love
And bring them safely through—
The faithful sun that rides above
Is not more loyal true—
They bear the lines or shame and sin,
The words of weal and woe;
And life itself is trusted in
The hands of Cobb and Co.

Their holdings stretch afar and wide
O'er range and blue-grass road—
They know them on the Queensland side,
All all their cheques are good;
Their drovers through the Border ply
South-east from Mulga town,
And whether tracks be green or dry
Their mobs are moving down—
While feeding with a half-mile spread
The lazy wethers go,
The notice reads: 'A thousand head
Of fats from Cobb and Co.'

The bullock-driver scarcely feels
His way on new cut track
Ere Cobb and Co., with lighter wheels,
Have run the marks out-back;
And while the seasons come and go
And through the changing years
All flags are dipped to Cobb and Co.,
The Western pioneers;
What reck if all the creeks are dry
And hot winds blight and blow,
We'll meet and fill our glasses high—
'Good luck to Cobb and Co.!'

(Cobb and Co.—Will H. Ogilvie, Glenrowan, 30 Mar 1895, p.4 & The Daily Telegraph, 6 Sep 1924, p.13)

Note: "Will H. Ogilvie, so well-known in the Molong, Parkes, and Forbes districts, who has been living at Kelso, Scotland, for some years, has been offered and accepted the position of bulletin editor at Iowa State College, U.S. Ogilvie has written some of the best verse ever done in Australia, and though perhaps he is not so popular amongst out-back readers as his contemporaries, ' Banjo' Patterson and Henry Lawson, his work, on the whole, has about it a better finish and richer ring. His 'Graves Out Back,' ' The Rose Out Of Beach,' ' Bowmont Water,' ' Fairy Tales,' ' To a Bunch of Heather,' and a host of other poems are pathetic of sentiment and sweet and musical as the water of a mountain rivulet. Ogilvie and ill-fated Harry Morant ('The Breaker') met together in Parkes years ago, and though from most points of view their natures were at variance, there was in common between them a sort of silent sympathy—for 'This Breaker' wrote love-sonnets and songs and much else that had about it a lot of merit." (Personal Pars, 14 Apr 1905, p.8)

Meanwhile "the historic Cobb and Co. coaches ... ran the gauntlet of bushrangers during the gold rush" years (Clapp: Railwayman with a one-track mind, 25 Aug 1945, p.10) and beyond. Their "encounters with the bushrangers would fill many a page of a thrilling book." (Cobb and Company, 22 Mar 1893, p.6)

11. THE BUSHRANGERS.–EDWARD H. MORGAN. BOWRAL

Rogue by heredity, felon by birth,
Ancestors often the scum of the earth;
Bred on 'duffed' mutton and other folks' beef;
Horse-stealer, brand-fakir, rowdy, and thief.

Rides like a centaur – no country too rough –
Lithe as a warrigal, wiry and tough;
Joined by a comrade, some human reproach,
Plucks up his courage and sticks up the coach.

Then becomes 'wanted,' and warrants abound;
Troopers are eager to run him to ground;
Aye, to be hunted and hounded his lot;
Finally hanged, or, if lucky, is shot.

Never the hero some writers aver,
Seldom the scoundrel his critics infer,
Two great attractions for men of his mould –
Lots of excitement and lightly-won gold.

(The Bushranger, 8 Feb 1896, p.10)

12. THE BUSHRANGERS' CAVE— ETHEL MILLS.

Such wattle, ah ! Such wattle ; it is golden as the sunlight
Which bathes the frowning rock-cliffs, where the white clematis showers
Its wealth of starry blossoms o'er the mosey granite ledges ;
But the wattle guards the secret with its tangled screen of flowers.
A secret ! Would you know it, you must part the guarding branches ;
Never step beyond the thicket, for scant foothold lies below,
Where a steep and jagged crevice guards the entrance to the stronghold
Where the outlaw braved the troopers half a century ago.
'Tis a cave where runs deep water past isolated boulders,
Not a place to choose to live in save when hope and luck has fled,
To be hushed to sleep by eddies as they whisper in the darkness
Tales of long-forgotten sunlight to the clustered bats o'erhead.
An eerie place, uncanny—let us up again to daylight ;

Let us leave these darksome waters where eyeless creatures dwell ;
But amid the wealth of blossoms and graceful twining creepers
We must shut our eyes to picture all this Heaven turned to Hell.
The flat below was sounding with the firing of the troopers,
The rocks above re-echoed as the deadly rifles rang ;
The powder-blackened faces were alight with lust of battle,
While below, unchanged, unheeding, the earth bound river sang.
'Short and merry life an outlaw's,' so the ancient ballads tell us ;
Short was his but scarcely merry when the flat below was red
With the blood of trusted comrades, while the hunters watched above him
For the quarry driven earthward with the price upon his head.
A man outlawed and hunted, watching there in utter darkness ;
A charge or two still left him, and an eye as true as steel,
And troopers only human you could scare expect they'd follow,
Where in unfamiliar darkness lurked the serpent for the heel.
Know some secret outlet, or, wounded, to some by-way
Creep away and die by inches, watched by greedy vampire eyes,
We shall never know ; the wattle guards the secrets of his passing,
And above the golden wattle all God's golden sunshine lies.

(Original Poetry—Ethel Mills, The Grange, Stanthorpe [Oct 13], 2 Jan 1897, p.42)

13. Farewell to W. Rochester–Hawkeye.

Dame Nature was garnering wattle of gold
Where many a watercourse flow'd,
Bright mornings of springtide were stretching away,
Field flowers were waking to greet a new day.
The magpies were wailing a sorrowful lay —
Wee birds on the wires had something to say
About Rochester leaving the road.

Far over the hill sounds a Cobb and Co. coach ;
It sways with a wonderful load.
But the passengers murmur a soft lullaby,
Though the glare of the west keeps hot in the eye.
And the end of that road's in the dip of the sky,
They knew all the ribbons were well handled by
Bill Rochester—King of the Road.

From west back to east is a wonderful stride ;
But necessity keeps no abode.
Far over the valley all horse coaches fade
Like wool-clipper ships when the anchors are weigh'd.
Yet early and late a good service has made
Bill Rochester King of the Road.

Often cold as if heaven had snow'd
A steady strong flutter of twelve miles an hour,
Through Coopernook dust or a web-footed shower ;
While patrons keep happy and chuckle 'more power'
To Bill Rochester—King of the Road.

Away from head office at break of the morn,
With ladies array'd 'a la mode' ;
Civility, method, precision and care,
One eye to the luggage and one to the fare ;
Till globe-trotting people are ready to swear
By Bill Rochester's King of the Road.

Those ratty new chaffeurs that gallop like mad
And never seem sure of the code ;
Piratical scorchers that scatter the drift,
And rush round the corners until her wheels lift ;
Such road hogs and puppies ! They never can shift
Bill Rochester—King of the Road.

When the last bag's delivered—the last tally sign'd ;
When the beauties of afternoon glow'd,
We'll claim a cool seating from dinner till dark,
Away from the dust in the trees of the park ;
And hear how the bushrangers got off the mark
From Bill Rochester—King of the Road.

Tell the new boss for certain, what ever his name ;
He can reap where another man sow'd.
Storekeepers and cockies and dealers in pie,
And schoolies and coolies let other cars fly—
We regulate watches and office clocks by
Bill Rochester—King of the Road.

(Farewell to W. Rochester, 28 Aug 1926, p.6)

"The romance of road-coaching in Australia ... abounds with incident and accident by flood and fell, by field and forest. Over miles of drought-stricken plains, through leagues of raging bush-fires, amid incessant rains and through the raging waters of swollen rivers, Cobb's coaches plunged along, beneath blazing sun-heat and in blinding storm, in heat and in cold, in midnight darkness and the crash of elemental war. The three great lamps have glowed in the blackest night as beacons of hope and messengers of civilisation, Cobb's mail-coach typifying a red link between the active world of affairs and the expatriated dwellers of the far Out-back." (A Pioneer of the Coaching Days: The Late James Rutherford, 20 Sep 1911, p.26)

14. Long Jim of Cobb & Co.–Bullman.

When he tells you of the leaders and the wheelers he has driven,
Of the colts that he has broken into harness—raw and green,
You can bet upon the box seat he's past master with the ribbons ;
He's the bean ideal of drivers, perhaps the best that you have seen.
To the rattling of the traces
And the creaking of the braces
He keeps the conversation going with consummate easy flow.
He knows all about 'crook' wagers, Handicaps, and weight-for-ages,
And he's just the very man to suit the firm of Cobb & Co.

He'll tell you fairy fables about snakes and of 'gohannas,'
About the girl who tends the parlor at the wayside public house ;
He'll discuss the team he's driving and the body horses names,
And the many frightened passengers on whom he's had to 'rouse.'
He gives the leaders just a feeler,
Put the double on the wheelers,
After which he soothes them softly with a 'gently boys, So ! Ho !'
And he shows the box seats whether He can pull his team together
And tool a five-horse coach along, does Jim of Cobb & Co.

He's full of information about the shearing at Glenaaring
And the fight between the big gun and the New Churn rouseabout.
He'll enlarge upon the method of pugilistic sparring,
And discuss with much minuteness what is styled a clean knock out.
He's a racy conversationalist.
Knows all about the pastoralist,
As he keeps his team right well in hand, For he drives the five you know.
And he'll always take a liquor, After which he gives a 'flipper'
To the lazy off-side wheeler, does Long Jim of Cobb & Co.

When he gets up to the shanty and the groom the horses changes,
And he gets his cup of coffee and his whisky and some scone,
It's 'garn-up there' with a whip crack, and he's off towards the ranges.
Yet he keeps good headway making
And he doesn't mind the shaking.
But the passengers will grumble ; he pretends he doesn't know,
For he smiles and gives a short cough As he knocks a cloud of flies off
That swarm around his horses, does Long Jim of Cobb & Co.

How he'll frighten nervous people with accounts of horses bolting,
About the crossing at the Barcoo where the horses have to swim,
And the coach capsize at Boulia, and of accidents revolting,
Where by special act of Providence he just Saved his 'gory' skin.
And you're all agog and gaping
At his easy way of taking
Such frightful, thrilling incidents; but now you're in the know.
You conclude he's devil me caring,
But you hardly keep from swearing
As he bumps you in a wheel rut, does Long Jim of Cobb & Co.

Then its lights, ho ! of the township. How the whip cracks at its glancing
Hound the heads of all five horses midst the rattle, for they must
Know the stage is over, and they reef almost to prancing
As they're drawn up to the office in a steam of sweat and dust.
All the people know the driver
And he's very much alive, Sir,
To the smiles of township beauties, for with them he's quite the beau,
For his coming some hearts gladden,
Ah ! and many too twill sadden,
For he carries good and bad news, does Long Jim of Cobb & Co.

All ! such good times for the driver, ah ! those roaring days of coaching,
And time rolls on right merrily, for life will ebb and flow.
But the liquor pressed upon him will ever keep encroaching,
And he's fast becoming sottish, for the people make him so.
If passengers who mean kindly
Could not thrust upon him blindly
The bottle, which to drivers is a dangerous, deadly foe,
But cease their invitations
To press on him potations
They'd not help to get him off the box of Messrs. Cobb & Co.

(The Poet's Corner—Bullman, Aramac Hospital, July 9, 20 Nov 1900, p.10)

Along the tracks of Cobb and Co. — The Roaring Days !

15. 'Old Jack' of Coaching Days– Marion Miller Knowles.

Lor', yes! my coaching days are 'done!' I'm but a worn-out horse
   That raced to win—but ended lame upon Life's stony course,
Time was when no one drove a coach with steadier hand than I ;
O'er rough or smooth—'twas in the blood—I made the horses fly.
   The townsfolk took a pride in me ; and I in my good name ;
   I never took a drop too much, whatever went or came.
Who bet their money then on Jack were safe—I mind me well,
They said I'd race 'Old Nick' himself to the very gates of hell!
And though, for years and years I played that game of pitch-and-toss ;
   Yet never once a beast died hard that owned me for its boss.
My heart was soft to helpless things—I'd a little girl, you see,
That always kept the balance straight between the road and me.
She knew the horses, every one, and called them all by name—
   'Boxer,' 'Trumps,' and 'Killaloe,' 'Old Ranger,' 'Bob,' and 'Game.'
   And never yet the coach was in, but she was standing there,
   With the light from out the stables like a glory on her hair.
Clap hands, clap hands!—my Daddy's home! she'd shout for very joy,
   And suit the action to the word, just like some merry boy.
   I loved her more than life itself—that little girl of mine!
She'd have made a better man than I square up, and 'toe the line.'
Her eyes were blue as heaven above ; her hair was rings of gold ;
   They used to say the like of her was never meant grow old.
Well, one wild winter came our way, and cut the roads up rough,
For once, I found work pretty stiff, and luck out, sure enough !
The trees were falling thick as leaves with every blast that blew,
   And many a tiring job I had to cut my passage through.

The flats were like a glue-pot ; but, driving rain or gale,
Late or early must arrive the Queen's own Royal Mail.
I was often late that season ; but no mortal could do more ;
Against such odds a ship in vain might strive to reach a shore.
And never captain loved his boat with stronger love than I
Loved that old coach of Cobb and Co.'s I pulled through wet or dry ;
And when my luck with her was out, it went with other things ;
My heart was soon enough to feel the whip-lash trouble flings.
My little one fell ill that year, she'd caught a feverish cold ;
The doctor said her case was bad, on life she'd little hold.
Night after night I hurried home, nigh choking with the load
That lay like iron on my breast the whole day on the road.
She loved to hear my voice, I knew, a singing her to sleep—
She'd never mind how loud it was; how rough-and coarse and deep!
My little maid, she leaned on me as trusting as a dove ;
She knew the height and breadth, you see, of her old father's love!
One morning when I had to go, she did not seem so bright,
But whispered, *I will clap my hands when you come home to-night!*
All day it rained without a break, and, on the journey back,
I saw a giant gum-tree fall right crash across the track.
I cursed my luck. The passenger on board was one-eyed Max—
A bent old fellow from the creek, who couldn't wield an axe.
So when at last I got a start, the night was drawing nigh—
I thought of my poor little one with many a weary sigh.
She'd find it hard to keep awake; her golden head would nod ;
I wondered that so fair a thing was sent to me from God.
I reached the town. It seemed to me all voices sounded queer.
Less hearty in their greetings—and my heart stood still with fear.
What's up ? I said. Jim Heywood spoke, his voice was hoarse and low—
Old chap, it hurts to tell you ; but—she died two hours ago.
Dead! Dead!—my bonny, little maid, I not by her side !
I swore at him for devil's spawn, him that he lied !
I made my way home up the hill my brain was in a whirl.
Ah, God! too true that she was gone, my own, dear little girl !
She'd fallen fast asleep without one last word from her Dad,
She'd asked for me 'till breath had failed'—my God, it sent me mad.
I bade them hold their babbling tongues, and leave me with my dead ;
My little one! too well I knew the sweet words she'd have said.
And though she could not hear my voice, I held her to my breast ;
And sang the songs I used to sing, the songs she loved the best.
And somehow then it seemed to me the white face of the child
Looked happier as I held her there, and even sweeter smiled.

* * *

That's many a long, long year ago!—I never thought to tell,
The sorrow of a worn-out heart that kept old secrets well !
I wish the Boss above would give His order for the track.
Where the old are let down lightly, and the tired ones don't go back.
I'm old and tired enough, He knows! No need to further roam—
Ah, God, to hear her clap her hands, and cry 'My Daddy's home !'

(Original Poetry 25 Jan 1908, p.51)

Cobb and Co. moved into New South Wales in 1862. "On Thursday the town of Bathurst was pleasurably excited by the arrival of the coaching 'plant' of the celebrated firm of Cobb and Co, of Melbourne ... We understand that arrangements on a very liberal scale will be made by the firm, with as little delay as possible, to convey passengers to and from the Metropolis and the respective diggings." (Sydney News, 3 Jul 1862, p.3) "With the most indefatigable industry, and extraordinary success, [James Rutherford] devoted himself to the organisation of the business of mail carrying in New South Wales and [later] Queensland, and it is said of Cobb and Co.—that is, of Mr Rutherford, who was the main spirit in the firm—that it opened roads where never else our railways would have penetrated." (The Founder of Cobb & Co., 12 Dec 1924, p.4)

16. THE WHIPS OF COBB AND CO.–AUTHOR UNKNOWN.

I've been coaching down in New South, riding in the Royal mail,
On the box in Vic and Tassy, on the boot in snow and hail ;
Riding in my sober senses, riding with my lamps alight,
Watching 'Jehu' with the ribbons, seeing if he held them right ;
Marked his pull and all his quiver ; marked the way he held the whip ;
Marked him try to do a straddle ; marked his liking for a nip ;
Marked his every blooming action ; marked his blooming cuddies, too ;
Marked his coach from rack to pole point ; as a critic ought to do.

And I've got him in the optic, I've got him in me mind,
As I've seen him whip the kiddies to the call of 'whip behind.'
And I feel him mount a boulder, fail to straddle when he ought,
Graze a stump and blame the wheeler, curse him when his whip got caught ;
Comb my whiskers with the branches, never thinks to 'pologise ;
Dumps me into ruts and gullies, shakes my innards in Gilgais.
And I mark him down as wanting, and his pace as extra slow—
Why he isn't even in it with the Queensland Cobb and Co.

So my mind goes harking backwards to the days of long ago,
Back to old familiar faces in the ranks of Cobb and Co.
And I see a whiskered chivvy—you can guess the 'chiv,' I mean—
It was known as Billy Mitchell ; is he still above the green?
Many miles I've ridden with him ; many yarns to me he's told ;
Many drinks we've had together—'ginger beer'—in days of old ;
Many times I've blown his bugle when we reached the sandy lane ;
Many times I've held the ribbons when we crossed the Myall Plain.

Harry Bruce and big Jack Warner, both were demons in the dark ;
They could drive their blooming carriage where a dingo couldn't bark.
They would never comb your whiskers with the branches overhead ;
And they'd 'break her' into gullies like a hearse that bore the dead.
The Andersons and Davy Teys, and Jim and Micky Carr,
Could steer a team through forest box or stunted coolabah ;
And Douglas, with his ready wit and ever-cheerful smile,
Would drive a team of five abreast, or five in single file.

Then my fancy turns to Rogers, good old Jimmy of that ilk ;
When he wasn't driving coaches he was mostly sporting silk.
Ride or drive, the same old Jimmy never fence was yet too high ;
And you never heard him grumble if the roads were wet or dry.
And Jimmy D—, you know the rest, he's on the Yeulba track,
A man to cheer a gloomy soul, or bring a wanderer back ;
A fair and square 'bontoshta,' an' a man I'm proud to know,
Is this more than brilliant unit in the ranks of Cobb and Co.

Last I saw of old Ted Manning, up in Longreach drawing beers—
Chucked the whip and leather ribbons—dealing in the cup that cheers.
Where, I wonder, are the others, Is their balance high or low?
Do they still convey the mail bags for Cobb and Co.?
For I miss 'em in my travels—little Dick, and Tom, and Fred ;
Some, I know, have left the coaches ; some to other lands have fled ;
Now and then I meet a rambler, and Tom had to let them go,
For the drought had played the devil with the whips of Cobb and Co.

Yes, I miss them, good old drivers, with cheerful 'get away' ;
It was good in sit beside 'em even on the wettest day.
It was good to hear their laughter, listen to the tales they told ;
May their years be long and happy 'ere they rest beneath the mould.
Seems as if the gods had chosen men like them to swing the whip
On the sun-scorched tracks of Queensland, where the only joy's a nip.
Never mind, ye western Jehus, in the end to Heaven you'll go
With your rein hand for a token that you wrought for Cobb and Co.

1925 Note: "So far as I can ascertain these verses have never been published previously, nor is the name of the author known. The verses were typewritten, and thumb worn—evidently they had been handled a good deal." (Cobb's Coaches, 17 Jan 1925, p.17)

17. TO MR PAT GOOLEY, OF MESSRS COBB AND CO.– J. ADDISON WHITE.

We miss the old coach, and the seven o'clock post,
With its letters and packets of news ;
The railway is gained, but how much, hath been lost,
Is a quantum for differing views.

Though the gathering crowd forgot, one and all,
To present you with tickets to banquet and ball,
We'll toast your good health in compliment true—
There's many a worse driver, believe me, than you.

Up hill, and down dale, and on dry, dusty level,
In hail, rain, and shine, you have driven us well ;
Often thirsty and heated—but well-mannered and civil :
A few eyes will moisten when we bid you farewell.

When down life's steep incline your chariot doth tend,
And the fast-flying coachman speeds to the end ;
Keep a steady look-out through the changing view,
And say, 'I am here !' when the Mailman is due.

When we, on our last trip, are called to embark,
When the daylight expires and the shadows grow dark :
May we 'fix up our lamps,' and 'all a-board !' take,
And 'pull up' at a grave with our foot on the brake.

(To Mr Pat Gooley, of Messrs Cobb and Co., 13 May 1886, p.3)

By the lst day of January, 1866 Cobb and Co. had expanded into Queensland. "Cobb & Co.'s Telegraph Line of Royal Mail Coaches will commence running for Ipswich and Toowoomba on Monday ... Booking Offices: Younge's Royal Hotel, North Brisbane and Royal Mail Hotel, South Brisbane," with horse-coaching lines running across Queensland for the following 58 years. (Classified Advertising, 29 Dec 1865 p.1) "Slowly but surely of late years the horse coach has been disappearing from many parts, of the State Queensland, until earlier in the week there appeared in our columns, that on August 14, the last horse-coach trip of the world-renowned firm of Cobb and Co. had been run from Surat to Yeulba ... The motor coach has come in its place, but memory of the old conditions will long survive." (The Last Coach, 5 Sep 1924, p.16)

18. Good-Bye to Cobb & Co.—Steve Hart.

No move across the salt bush plains, through Mulga clumps and Yarran,
The old red coach no longer strains across the ridges barren.
How oft, in little lawns out back, we'd watch it come and go,
With straining eyes along the track, to welcome Cobb and Co.

No more we'll see it rushing down the steep and rocky ranges;
For where it went soon grew a town, about the old horse changes.
Still out it pushed to no man's land, thru' dusk and dawn's grey glow,
It made the tracks through hills of sand, the coach of Cobb and Co.

No more through townships once a week, past squatters and selectors;
To fossickers along the creek, up hills to old prospectors.
Through forests thick it blazed the trails, and always sure if slow;
To lonely men it brought the mails, The coach of Cobb and Co.

No more in sunshine, or in rain, no more in rivers flooded,
We'll ever see such teams again, by pure bred sires blooded.
The railway lines pushed further out, the old-time coach must go.
Now motor cars which fear no drought, displaces Cobb and Co.

But memory will oft fly back, when cars fast by are dashing,
We'll miss the drivers' old whip crack, and see bright headlights flashing.
And far out where my old mates lie, they'll see pass to and fro,
A silent team go slowly by, the ghosts of Cobb and Co.

(Good-Bye to Cobb & Co, 5 Sep 1924, p.4)

19. THE GHOSTS OF COBB AND CO.–AUTHOR UNKNOWN.

I hear the shouts of coaches 'out,'
Whip cracks and straining traces ;
The clanging bars, the driver's shout,
The creak of the thoroughbraces.
At Running Stream and Cudgegong,
I see the headlights show ;
And list to the travellers' happy song,
Who ride on Cobb and Co.

(Coaching and the Coaching Days, 13 Feb 1934, p.4)

20. Shadow Of Cobb & Co.—Hugh Stone.

It stands beside an old cow bail,
   Where tied-up Rover howls ;
A coach that was the Royal Mail
   A roosting place for fowls;
A special perch has a Leghorn,
   A Langshan roosts below;
A crowing couple ev'ry morn
   From off a Cobb & Co.

Along the back a Spanish hen
   Mates with a Wyandotte,
Though a big Dorking now and then
   Disputes the black bird's spot.
And when long shadows speak the sun
   Its setting time doth show,
On the box seat an Orpington
   Roosts high on Cobb & Co.

And there it stands of glory shorn
   That was a driver's pride
When creaking past the fields of corn
   It made the mountain side,
Or moved o'er plains with flashing lights
   That set the track aglow
When through the mud on winter's nights
   It splashed for Cobb & Co.

Now 'gone the days' when its four wheels
   Went rumbling down the road,
Or through the bush when 'Jack's' loud peals
   Greeted its human load.
The lamps are smashed that gleamed afar,
   Its axles bent and low:
'Base uses' since the motor car
   Disposed of Cobb & Co.

I sit and look at it sadly,
   A battered thing on wheels,
No leaders pulling reins madly.
   No polers lashing heels,
No driver with his vice-like grip
   Waiting the word to go,
No 'All aboard!' no cracking whip—
   Shadow of Cobb & Co.

(Shadow of Cobb and Co., 10 Sep 1925, p.18)

"The last coach owned by Cobb and Co., now being used between Yeulba and Surat, in Queensland, will be replaced by a motor car next month." (Topical Talk, 27 Aug 1924, p.10)

21. THE LAST COACH–R.J.C.

Good-bye, good-bye to Old Romance,
That marked the dusty roads—
Or watery, muddy roads perchance—
When each old creaking circumstance
Lurched onward with its loads.

Oh! Those were days when life was good,
Despite the jolts and jars ;
When each his coach-mate understood,
And linked up in a brotherhood
Behind the swingle-bars.

By day and night the coaches went
Where trains were but a dream,
But they were times in gladness spent
By those on fun or fortune bent,
Drawn by the sweating team.

The motor cars now hold the sway,
And all your hopes are vain ;
But never mind, old coach, for they
May in the future time give way
To the buzzing aeroplane.

(Topical Talk, 27 Aug 1924, p.10)

22. The Lights of Cobb & Co.—Henry Lawson

Fire lighted, on the table a meal for sleepy men,
A lantern in the stable, a jingle now and then ;
The mail-coach looming darkly by light of moon and star,
The growl of sleepy voices — a candle in the bar ;
A stumble in the passage of folk with wits abroad ;
A swear-word from a bedroom — the shout of 'All aboard!'
'Tchk-tchk! Git-up!' 'Hold fast, there!' and down the range we go;
Five hundred miles of scattered camps will watch for Cobb and Co.

Old coaching towns already 'decaying for their sins,'
Uncounted 'Half-Way Houses,' and scores of 'Ten Mile Inns' ;
The riders from the stations by lonely granite peaks ;
The black-boy for the shepherds on sheep and cattle creeks ;
The roaring camps of Gulgong, and many a 'Digger's Rest' ;
The diggers on the Lachlan ; the huts of Farthest West ;
Some twenty thousand exiles who sailed for weal or woe ;
The bravest hearts of twenty lands will wait for Cobb and Co.

The morning star has vanished, the frost and fog are gone,
In one of those grand mornings which but on mountains dawn ;
A flask of friendly whisky—each other's hopes we share—
And throw our top-coats open to drink the mountain air.
The roads are rare to travel, and life seems all complete ;
The grind of wheels on gravel, the trot of horses' feet,
The trot, trot, trot and canter, as down the spur we go—
The green sweeps to horizons blue that call for Cobb and Co.

We take a bright girl actress through western dust and damps,
To bear the home-world message, and sing for sinful camps,
To wake the hearts and break them, wild hearts that hope and ache—
(Ah! when she thinks of those days her own must nearly break !)
Five miles this side the gold-field, a loud, triumphant shout :
Five hundred cheering diggers have snatched the horses out,
With 'Auld Lang Syne' in chorus through roaring camps they go—
That cheer for her, and cheer for Home, and cheer for Cobb and Co.

Three lamps above the ridges and gorges dark and deep,
A flash on sandstone cuttings where sheer the sidings sweep,
A flash on shrouded waggons, on water ghastly white ;
Weird bush and scattered remnants of 'rushes' in the night ;
Across the swollen river a flash beyond the ford :
'Ride hard to warn the driver ! He's drunk or mad, good Lord !'
But on the bank to westward a broad, triumphant glow—
A hundred miles shall see to-night the lights of Cobb and Co. !

Swift scramble up the siding where teams climb inch by inch ;
Pause, bird-like, on the summit—then breakneck down the 'pinch' !
Past haunted half-way houses—where convicts made the bricks—
Scrub-yards and new bark shanties, we dash with five and six—
By clear, ridge-country rivers, and gaps where tracks run high,
Where waits the lonely horseman, cut clear against the sky ;
Through stringy-bark and blue-gum, and box and pine we go ;
New camps are stretching 'cross the plains the routes of Cobb and Co.

Throw down the reins, old driver—there's no one left to shout ;
The ruined inn's survivor must take the horses out.
A poor old coach hereafter !—we're lost to all such things—
No bursts of songs or laughter shall shake your leathern springs.
When creeping in unnoticed by railway sidings drear,
Or left in yards for lumber, decaying with the year—
Oh, who'll think how in those days when distant fields were broad
You raced across the Lachlan side with twenty-five on board.

Not all the ships that sail away since Roaring Days are done—
Not all the boats that steam from port, nor all the trains that run,
Shall take such hopes and loyal hearts—for men shall never know
Such days as when the Royal Mail was run by Cobb and Co.
The 'greyhounds' race across the sea, the 'special' cleaves the haze,
But these seem dull and slow compared with bygone Roaring Days !
The eyes that watched are dim with age, and souls are weak and slow,
The hearts are dust or hardened now that broke for Cobb and Co.

(Christmas Number of The Bulletin, 11 Dec 1897, p.9)

AULD LANG SYNE.

1892 Note: "Auld Lang Syne ... Hogg and Motherwell say : — We subjoin the earliest copy of this song that we have ever met with, taken from a broadside printed before 1700, from which it will be seen that notwithstanding the poet's resolute disclaimer, the merits of his version are peculiarly his own : —

Should auld acquaintance be forgot And never thought upon,
The flames of love extinguished And freely passed and gone ;
Is thy kind heart now grown so cold In that loving breast of thine,
That thou canst never once reflect On auld lang syne.

Where are thy protestations— Thy vows and oaths, my dear,
Thou made to me and I to thee In register yet clear ?
Is faith and truth so violate To the immortal gods divine,
That thou canst never once reflect On auld lang syne !

Is't Cupid's fears or frostie cares That makes the sp'rits decay ?
Or is't some object of more worth That's stolen thy heart away ?
Or some desert makes thee neglect Her once so much was thine,
That thou canst never once reflect On auld lang syne.

Is't worldly cares so desperate That makes thee to despair ?
Is't that makes thee exasperate, And makes thee to forbear ?
If thou of that were free as I, Thou surely should be mine ;
And then of new we would renew Kind auld lang syne.

But since that nothing can prevail And all hope now is vain,
Prom these rejected eyes of mine Still showers of tears shall rain ;
And thou that hast me now forgot Yet I'll continue thine,
Yea, thou that hast me now forgot A nd auld lang syne.

If ere I have a house, my dear, That's truly called mine,
And can afford but country cheer Or aught that's good therein ;
Though thou were rebel to the king, And beat with wind and rain,
Thou'rt sure thyself of welcome, love, For auld lang syne.

In his letter to Mrs. Dunlop, in December 1788, Burns speaks of this song as one that had often thrilled through his soul, and exclaims, *Light be the turf on the Heaven-inspired poet who composed this Heaven-inspired fragment. There is more of the fire of native genuis in it than in half-a-dozen of modern English Bacchanalians."* (Auld Lang Syne, 1 Oct 1892, p.13) While the song sung in 1887 was as follows:

AULD LANG SYNE.

Should auld acquaintance be forgot,
And never brought to mind?
Ah, never ; to this day I've got
That little note you signed.

And often, often, I have thought
Much cheaper 'twould have been,
If, when you wrote that little note,
You'd stencilled it in tin.

We twa hae skulkit in the fields,
For watermelons fine,
But at the fashions farmer's voice,
We fled; and made no sign.

So now, tae ferlie diel's awa,
Syne hurdies warstna paiks,
Blythe dourlach gudeman usquebaugh,
Hech, mon, ilk nainsel aiks.

(Auld Lang Syne, 8 Oct 1887, p. 2)

23. The Days of Cobb and Co.–G. M. Smith.

We have telephones and cables
 And electric telegraph
To flash the news to any point
 In a minute and a half.
To sum it up what way you will,
 It's anything but slow ;
It seems a vast improvement
 On the days of Cobb and Co.

We have electric trams and Cable trams,
 The motor and the bike ;
You can get about the country now
 At any speed you like.
We have railways to the back blocks,
 Where the iron horses go,
And yet the times were better
 In the days of Cobb and Co.

There was enterprise and money
 And any amount of work.
There was wool and fat stock rolling in
From the Mitchell plains round Bourke ;
There was merchandise and passengers
 To carry to and fro ;
There was life too, in Australia,
 In the days of Cobb and Co.

To travel out a thousand miles
 You'd book yourself in town ;
They'd guarantee to pull you through
 When you paid your money down.
They travelled then by rough bush tracks,
 Through mountains, bog and snow,
They'd set you down well up to time,
 Would good old Cobb and Co.

And they had some clever drivers,
 Who could handle horses neat ;
To see them work their ribbons on
 Those bush tracks was a treat.
They would get a change of coaches
 Every twenty miles or so,
And they drove some slashing horses
 In the days of Cobb and Co.

Our progress has been rapid,
 But the days are poorer now
Than the days of Jimmy Tyson
 And Good old Jackey Dow.
I remember well the sixties,
 And transit then was slow ;
But give to me the golden days—
 The days of Cobb and Co.

(The Days of Cobb and Co., 5 Oct 1904, p.3)

24. THE DAYS OF COBB & CO.–WILLIAM MUGGRIDGE

I dream of the good old coaching days,
Of the grand old long-ago ;
Of the joyful ride — a seat outside —
On the coach of Cobb & Co.;
Of the music of the swingle-bars
And the merry hoof-taps, too;
When the leather springs were wonder things,
And the year-old things were new.

When the emu and the kangaroo
Fled across the unmade track,
As we went along; and the driver's song
Awakened the old out-back.
Ah, the horses then blazed coaching ways,
And carried the pioneer.
Then the bush was wide.
The far outside
Nowadays is brought too near.

The railway train and the motor car
Have hustled the coach away
To Phantom Land, where, I understand,
All the good things will stay ;
Away at the end of life's mirage,
In that far-off promised land,
Where swingle-bars — not motor cars —
Give joy to the happy band.

To the happy band of good old days,
To the days of Cobb & Co.,
I lift my glass as I toast The Pass
Into which the old days go.
Ah, soon I shall see the phantom coach,
And secure a seat outside ;
Then through The Gate, where old friends wait,
On a Cobb & Co. I'll ride.

(The Days of Cobb & Co., 8 Feb 1924, p.3)

25. IN THE DAYS OF COBB AND CO.—JACK MOSES

It does one good to knock around
And see our fertile lands,
Just waiting for the golden hour
To come from willing hands.

We should strive by might and main
To hold our precious prize,
To live in peace and harmony,
Beneath our sunny skies.

Think of those who have passed away,
They grubbed the great gum trees
They blazed the track with fire and axe,
All for you and me.

I hear the thrush on the mountain top,
And the settler's axe below,
Those were the times of grit and graft,
In the days of Cobb and Co.

(In the Days of Cobb and Co., 18 Nov 1931, p.4)

Along the tracks of Cobb and Co. — The Roaring Days !

Part Three

100 years on–
Presentation by Hazel Johnson

The following Presentation was delivered during the Surat-Yuleba Cobb and Co. Festival, 16-26 August 2024, celebrating 100 years since "the last horse-coach trip of the world-renowned firm of Cobb and Co. has been run from Surat to Yeulba."

The Presentation was attended by Her Excellency the Honourable Dr Jeannette Young AC PSM, Governor of Queensland, Professor Nimmo and other distinguished guests.

> "To travel out a thousand miles
> You'd book yourself in town ;
> They'd guarantee to pull you through,
> When you paid your money down.
> They travelled then by rough bush tracks,
> Through mountains, bog and snow,
> And deliver you well up to time,
> Would good old Cobb & Co.
> And they had some splendid drivers,
> Who could handle horses neat ;
> To see them work their ribbons on
> Those bush tracks was a treat.
> And they'd get a change of coaches
> Every twenty miles or so ;
> And they drove some slashing cattle
> In the days of Cobb & Co."

Just imagine, with a merry rattle, trot, trot, clicketty clack, "the galloping horses and swaying coach that spun past ... with a cracking of whips ... in a rallying sprint to land the mails on time ... at the little post office" in Surat. Leaving St. George ... the five horses ... with never a protest ... swung the coach out by the new hotel and rumbled through the silent terrace to the Post Office ... where bags and packages were rolled down the steps ... and packed in boot and rear ... for delivery along the road to Surat ... 80 miles distant ... then Yeulba, and Brisbane. But first a call at Cobb and Co.'s booking office and store, where more packages were obtained ... The team of five, fine, white horses were well handled by driver Rawley Sting."

- In Surat it appears that after being a 'post town' "a post office was established in 1852 ..."
- 1919 "saw Mr & Mrs Clarke as the post office residents ... "
- By 1927 "attention was drawn to the inadequacy of the out-of-date post office, built at Surat over 50 years ago" and in 1937 "The post office building having been completed by Mr. Bell, the staff will occupy the premises this week-end. The new office fills a long-felt public need."
- And for those of you who love statistics ... how many miles do you think was covered in 1868 delivering mail in Queensland ... "950,488 miles were covered delivering mail in Qld ... more than double what it was just 4 years earlier."

Welcome Your Excellency, Mayor Wendy Taylor, Deputy Mayor Cameron O'Neil, councillors and history lovers, thank you all for gathering in Surat & Yuleba to celebrate the centennial of the last Cobb and Co. coach that ran in Qld and perhaps Australia. I believe celebrating all people who have built or fought for this great nation is vital—they certainly have my admiration and respect—without their 'unyielding courage, determination and resilience' Australia may not be the lucky country.

And I believe no Australian history is complete without the story of the great firm of Cobb and

Co. Written in 1923 "The era when the name of Cobb & Co. was a household word in New South Wales and Queensland is certainly gone—gone with all its glamor and glory of flash horses and wonderful feats of driving. Very few persons, except those who actually lived in the past, can have any idea what Cobb and Co. meant to the great outback. It carried to the families living in those lonely parts their letters and newspapers, to say nothing of numerous parcels ... and now and then a stray friend. This great work was done with wonderful regularity, and especially so considering the troubles and worries that had to be faced. The arrival of the coach in bush towns (like Yuleba and Surat) was the event of the week ... and its coming was eagerly awaited by the whole population, whose census could almost be taken at the post office soon after the event. The well-known rattle of wheels stirred to life and activity the most lethargic inhabitants. The news of the world, the local gossip as outlined in the newspapers ... (like the wedding in Springsure between a Blackall saddler and a Springsure barmaid, after only two days courtship) ... was printed in towns hundreds of miles away and messages from friends far distant, were symbolised in that often heard and truly welcome rumble."

Now 100 years on ... I am going to give you a glimpse of the 'unyielding courage, determination and resilience', from those who have come before us. Traits which helped create modern Australia. Traits which are just as valuable today as they were back then.

But first, let's pretend we are at the cricket and see how well you can do a Mexican wave ... now this group is going to represent Victoria, small group South Australia, New South Wales, Queensland and Western Australia ... note no Tasmania or Northern Territory groups ... This is pretty much how Cobb and Co. moved through Australia ... like a wave. Ever on the look-out for 'fresh fields,' "the Cobb and Company's telegraph line was extended to many places" but of course it was the 'iron horse' (or the railway) that kept the great commercial enterprise on the move and was "the last straw that brought this famous company to an end" ... of course along with the motor buggy!

Speaking of the railway ... let me share a funny story ... remembering there was no Google in 1877 ... or even 1977 for that matter ... "An amusing incident occurred at Sandy Creek the other day ... A girl, who had never before seen a railway train, observed one approaching, and fearful that a fluttering of clothes, hung out on a line to dry ... might frighten the engine. She ran to a man who was working close by, and asked if such would be the case. He laughingly replied in the affirmative ... but the girl was not satisfied, and asked the landlady of the hotel the same question. Seeing the fun of the thing she also answered 'yes,' ... whereupon, to her great astonishment ... the girl cut down the line, letting the clean linen fall into the mud. Although rather annoyed at the result of the joke ... she could not blame the girl, and could ... but indulge in a hearty laugh."

Now who exactly was Cobb and Co.? Cobb and Co. is a story that started with Adams & Co., express carriers, who came to Melbourne from America ... but if you wish, you can read about that at your leisure in my book series ... Let's skip to the renowned American, Freeman Cobb—he along with James Swanson, John Lamber, and John Murray Peck—finding that there was a demand for conveyance to the newly broken-out-diggings formed themselves into a company, Cobb and Co., running the American Telegraph Line of Coaches, in 1854 between Melbourne, Forest Creek and Bendigo.

By 1859 "no one, not even Cobb himself, imagined that his enterprise would so rapidly approach the magnificent development lately witnessed ... when the humble half dozen passenger conveyance ... was now represented by a gigantic car, holding fifty travellers and harnessed to fourteen greys ... as fine specimens of horse flesh as one can hope to find in the southern hemisphere ... 'tooled' by whips (drivers) who are equalled by few, and excelled by none."

However, having said that, some sources say it was actually the Cobb brothers, Freeman & Elisha Winslow Cobb, who commenced Cobb and Co.

Either way "They were the palmy days of Cobb's coaches! ... One by one they have left, these hardy, pioneers of the road, these men who recked not of danger, who smiled in the face of difficulties ... who calmly looked at impossibilities and overcame them. Furious driving, I grant you ... a reckless disregard, sometimes of their own and the passengers' necks ... probably. But what else could have been done, let me ask. There was no time to be shilly-shallying on the edge of a swamp—no use hesitating at taking a header down a steep gully with a broken boulder or slimy bottom. It was a shake of the reins, a crack of the stinging whipcord, a heigh ! ho! houp la ! a mad plunge, a creaking of springs, a straining of harness, a flying of mud and gravel ... and a get out on the other side at full gallop ... for you know her Majesty's mails must not be delayed ... One by one, I say, have these pioneers, of the road quitted."

In fact, there were many proprietors who ran under the 'style of Cobb and Co.', perhaps a rather boring read if you are not a descendant but exciting if it has been passed down through the generations that your great, great grandfather was a Cobb and Co. proprietor. With a show of hands, is there anyone here today whose ancestors were part of the Cobb and Co. enterprise or 'bailed-up' by bushrangers such as the Tamworth bushranger ... It was in 1874 that the Tamworth highway man was actually captured near Murilla Creek about half a mile from the Surat road. He was captured in a Shepherd's hut ... and "in his possession of a pack of cards, two counterfeit sovereigns (very bad imitations), and two flash counterfeit notes", among a few other things.

Back to the Cobb and Co. proprietors ... A. W. Robertson and John Wagner were the big players in Victoria while it was the mighty James Rutherford, Whitney, Hall & Bradley who brought coaching this far north, but there are many, many others. You may again read about them at your leisure in my 'Along the tracks of Cobb and Co' Book Series.

One of the lesser known proprietor was William Brown Bradley—I believe a man of determination ... this is one of his stories ... 1868 "Bradley says :—About the 9th of April last, with a buggy and two horses, I started for back country belonging to us south of the Darling ... a distance of eighty miles without water. I had horses I depended on, but after going thirty miles through the bush one of them knocked up and I had to camp ... I had only two bottles of water, which were now consumed ... Having no compass ... I started next morning, one horse still very well, and went about seven miles when I believed myself too much to the east. I changed my course due south ... or what I supposed south, and travelled forty or fifty miles, and found myself among mountains ... which caused me to admit that I was in unknown country ; and had no water. (We would call that lost!) The day had been very warm, and a painful sensation in the throat and tongue was felt; the horse was completely done ; here I camped. By daybreak I was after the horses, and found they had left me in the night ; found their tracks and with much toil (for I had eaten nothing since I started) ... followed them for ten miles ... About ten o'clock I came up to my best horse, the other nowhere to be seen ; and being in a fainting state from thirst, opened with my knife the neck vein, and drank more than a quart of my horse's blood. This horrible draught gave me much relief, but it was voided almost as soon as taken ... About 3 o'clock I found a kurrajong tree, and as well as I was able—for my knees trembled and my arms felt powerless—stripped away some of its bark, which I chewed, and found the sweet moisture of much benefit in clearing my throat and tongue ... and I felt convinced should anyone be in the like strait ... and have strength to procure plenty of this bark ... it would preserve life for a day or two. At 4 p.m. I again drank blood with exactly the same result ; my poor horse, Sydney, was now literally staggering ... All day it had been very hot, but at night it became quite cool, and I resolved to long-hobble my horse and follow him ... the reason of my hobbling him was that, weak as he was, he could out-walk me ... and even then I had to follow the sound of the chains. After going about six miles thus, he started into a reeling canter and stopped in a dry creek ... here I knew where I was ... ten miles had now to be got over, which took me about seven hours, when I reached one of my own tanks ... The horse, likewise found the tank, drank, rolled, and died ... the other horse got in the next day, and plunging headlong into the water, was drowned."

What a difference a mobile phone would have made in 1868! Sheer determination was evident not only when travelling but when manning the change stations—there is a story about a young man at a horse change who never saw anyone for two years, except those on the Cobb and Co. coach.

Speaking of travelling, if you wanted to reach here or beyond, travelling on Cobb and Co.'s Telegraph Line of Royal Mail Coaches, first you would need to buy your ticket ... "On one occasion, when the coach was loaded heavily, a passenger said to the driver, How come it is that you have three classes of passengers and three prices? We all seem to be crammed to suffocation. You'll pretty soon get to know all about it, said the driver ... First-class passengers will keep their seats; second-class will get out and walk to the top of the hill; third-class will walk and push the coach."

Next you need to know where the coaches leave from, such as ...

- Younge's Royal Hotel, North Brisbane
- Royal Mail Hotel, South Brisbane
- Phillips' Australian Hotel, Queen Street, or
- Witty's Imperial Hotel, Brisbane ...
- In Ipswich Hanran's North Star Hotel, Tattersall's Hotel ...
- Mr. Fraser's Queen's Arms, The Albion or the Royal Hotels, were departure places in Toowoomba ...
- While in Dalby ... The Criterion or The Royal Hotel ...
- Sportsman's Hotel, Warra
- Winieke's Eulba Hotel, The Sovereign Hotel & The Kangaroo Hotel, also Yuleba ...
- Roma departure places included Crosbie's Commercial Hotel, The Royal Hotel/ The Royal Mail Hotel
- And here in Surat, Tara's Hall Hotel ... while it is stated in 1880 that The Traveller's Inn was the first public-house in Surat, being changed to The Commercial by Mr. Naylor.

But of course, progress continued during this era and by 1876, you could travel Brisbane to Dalby via the iron horse (train), then by Cobb and Co. coach to Condamine, Yuelba, Surat, Roma, Mitchell, Charleville or further to Adavale, Thargomindah, Blackall ... in fact right up through the centre of Queensland ...

Now speaking of hotels or pubs, does anyone know which hotel burnt down in Roma in 1870, 1915, 1917 & 1919? [Yes, The Royal Hotel] ... Here is one of my favourite hotel/pub stories "A SNAKE YARN.—According to a Northern contemporary (and these tropical papers hardly ever tell tarradiddles) man rushed into a pub on the banks of the Burdekin one day last week, yelling for help. Soon it was ascertained that a fair sized black snake had crawled up inside one leg of his trousers. Willing hands helped the victim, and the reptile was, when extricated, found dead. As the man had felt many punctures, he was dosed with brandy for the following two days, and then danger being past, tended like a prince for the rest of the week, at the end of which time he took up his swag and proceeded on his lonely tramp. A few days after ... the driver of Cobb's coach dropped in and, being told the tale, knocked the public into extravagant profanity by explaining that the man had played the same game at fully a dozen pubs and shanties along the road. The plan the gentle boozer adopted was to find a snake, kill it, and when in sight of a pub, lodge it in his trousers."

If it actually had bitten him, the advice in 1912 was "to scarify and suck the wound", while giving "strychnine and alcohol showed no advantage". Another story tells of a Mrs Hammon "who felt something bite her toe, and looking down she discovered a large snake ... so she got a young man that happened to be there at the time to chop off one of the small toes, together with a portion of the outside of the left foot ... He had to repeat the blow four times before he took the piece clean off." It just makes you shudder, doesn't it!

Now back on the coach ... Perhaps safer than being bitten by a snake ... Part of a journey between Roma and Charleville was once described as follows: "The air at this time was not very cold, but crisp and delightful and the moon, like a globe of silver hung straight before us, simmering gently on the tree tops, and lighting up the avenues through which we dashed. Wrapped in our overcoats and mufflers, and bound round with rugs, a gentle glow suffused our bodies, and the drive proved most enjoyable. Bloomfield, as a driver, is one not easily surpassed. The manner in which he tooled the six splendid animals round trees and stumps, over logs, ruts, and stones, went far to confirm us in the generally expressed opinion ... that he is one of the best drivers King Cobb has in his employ. On the road we passed numerous teams, some laden with wool, others with produce, and the flames from the camp fires flickered and fell, casting grotesque shadows that danced among the trees weirdly. But the moon soon disappeared, and the ghostly dawn with its grim light came in succession, bringing with it a keen cold that made the flesh on one's face tingle. And when the great golden sun arose a pleasant warmth was quickly diffused among the chattering and shivering travellers, and later on ... beads of perspiration stood on the foreheads of those on the box. The light of day, however, displayed a saddening panorama. Nothing before us but a dreary stretch of road ... nothing on each side but barren ground as bare as a beach as far as grass was concerned ... and covered with the mournful murmuring mulga-tree. Past this ground, past bleachening bones, past poor thin and worn looking cattle, with a sky of brass overhead, and burning, blazing sun still on the patient animals, drew us until night fell, and again the moon rose With a mysterious splendour Touching the sombre leaves ... Still on we flew, and after 8 o'clock darted up the wide street of Charleville."

On other trips the descriptions included:
- "I felt as hot as two furnaces", and "the man that invented water-bags ought to have a front seat in heaven",
- "everything dry as dust" while "we traded in our horses, brought three, and broke in one in about five minutes",

or
- "to Euleba, the worst 16 miles of bad roads I wish to travel over", and
- "Charleville to Roma ... we did the journey comfortably in three days!"

I wonder if the children ever said "Are we there yet?"

Of course, no talk would be complete without a reference to the box seat. Some of your ancestors may have travelled the track along the western run from Brisbane to Adavale or to other places in Australia, on the box seat. 1875 "I have travelled many a mile with Cobb, always when I could, on Cobb's box. What special charm there is in a box-seat ... It is certainly not the most comfortable position in the coach, exposed as it is to the broiling heat and choking dust of summer, and the piercing wind, rain and sleet of winter. And yet it has a charm, for who would brook to ride inside when by fair means or by foul, by force or by guile, by pre-emptive right or by open or covert bribery, he could beg, borrow or steal the dignity of a box seat ?" Please note in Victoria "No ladies were allowed on the Box Seat of the Coach … 40 shilling fine for driver breaking this rule" … but we can be a little more lenient with the rules here in Queensland …

Now the question is, Are you sitting on the box seat today? [Prize given]

Now let's talk 'unyielding courage'—anything to do with snakes, I believe, requires 'unyielding courage'. A story about driver Charlie Snell and yes more snakes … although I did think about sharing the story of when a startled lizard ran up the legs of one of the horses, causing a bolt and a smash-up against a tree. About the only thing, that escaped unhurt was the gohanna …

But back to Charlie's story "When the snow commences to melt at the head of the Murray, there is trouble for the mail contractor running along these rivers … The rivers overflow their banks, always by way of creeks or billabongs, which often become too deep to cross … Sometimes great risks are taken by drivers in crossing these places rather than going around. All mails, etc., and passengers had to be put above the water line on top of the coach. I remember one incident in particular … This part of the Murray, I should think, would compare favorably with any other part of the world for snakes. They are there in thousands … in the long buffalo sort of grass that covers the Murray flats. On this particular morning we stopped at one of these flooded creeks … Only the driver and myself were aboard … and when the former surveyed the rise in water since he had previously, crossed, he remarked: It's a bit risky today, but I think we can get across … Just while we were making everything fast on the coach top, about a dozen snakes came out of the grass on to the road just in front and about the horses … Snell, a bit of a wag, looked at them, and said: No mail for you today, gentlemen, and turning to me, added: I get a visit from this crowd every day. You will see some of them will escort us across the water. And sure enough they did. As the horses walked into the water half a dozen of the snakes also, wriggled in, and swam across ahead of us, some turning back and others going right across." Definitely a time for courage with both the flooded rivers and the snakes!

Speaking of flooding, in 1877 "At Charleville, the Warrego rose, a height unknown for years past. We are sorry to learn that the carcasses of hundreds of sheep and cattle floated past Charleville in the early part of the week. The animals had evidently been located on low ground … and being most probably in low condition … the flood had washed them away before they could get to higher land."

While "Mails from Surat will be exchanged on the road. Handrails of the bridge at Surat visible." And in 1884 "The Commissioner of Police has received a telegram from Roma … that Cobb's coach, while attempting to cross the Balonne at St. George, on Saturday night, was swept down the river, the four horses bring drowned. The driver, after being an hour in the water, was saved. There were no passengers in the coach." They certainly didn't consider "If its flooded, forget it", nor did some support the old adage "Don't panic. That's the first rule of survival."

This is just one example from the 1800s … "DEATH OF A YOUNG LADY NAMED EMILY JANE M'GUIRE. It appears the mail, upon leaving Mudgee, had two lady passengers … and a male passenger … who sat upon the box with the driver. Arriving at Home Rule, the owner and driver requested the above gentleman to hold the reins while he delivered the mails, and he consented to do so ; but while the driver was engaged, he left, having requested another to hold the horses ... The flapping of the curtains, it is supposed, startled the horses, and they went away at full speed ... The horses at a rapid rate crossed the bridge, and, when within one mile ... the young lady ... made a jump from the coach, falling in such a manner that her neck was broken. Every assistance was rendered, but of no avail; life had passed. The horses proceeded at their leisure, and were stopped about half-way between the two towns."

In fact, many of our sayings have a long history, for example:
- Hell for leather:

"on one occasion just as the ostler released the new team, the offside leader started rearing, and finally bolted ... 'hell for leather' down the hill ... temporary easing of the pace enabled Andy to regain control of the team."
- Helter skelter:

1906 "the ponies were ... placed in Cobb & Co. stables. They managed, however, to slip their halters just as the train steamed into the platform, and bolted ... turning into the scrub ... Mr. Collins and Shirley Dwyer went helter-skelter in pursuit, and the little spirited greys were captured ... The fugitives were brought back to the stables"
- All good things apparently come to those who wait long enough:

"Word has been received that a new post office and postmaster's residence is assured for Surat. All good things apparently come to those who wait long enough. Surat residents are more patient than those of most inland towns, otherwise they would be clamouring for the completion of the main road to Glenmorgan, still 14 miles distant, with no work carried out for well over a year. No town in the State is more deserving of an all-weather road than Surat, which has not received many favours from the different Governments, either State or Federal."

And as for the spelling ... I untangled that journey of Yuleba at last Sunday's Cobb and Co.'s descendants gathering ...

Having said all that, the trait which I admire most in people from the past or today is resilience. The ability to 'bounce back' from difficult experiences—although it is apparently no longer called a trait but something that can be learnt or developed. Either way, clearly, the grand old days of Cobb and Co. were not "all romance and high adventure" but times when you had to be resilient, especially when travelling on a Cobb and Co. coach. We read "The ringing, swinging music of pattering hoofs, and the rattling jingle of harness sounds merry in our ears." While perhaps a more accurate description is the one written in 1855 "what a terrible noise the coach makes, I hope we shall have no accident ... they dash through a deep mud hole. Bump goes every head nearly to the ceiling of the coach, and down comes everyone upon his seat ... and then the new passenger, a lucky digger, jumps in and takes his seat. Away go the prads as before at a rattling pace. The bumps are occasionally almost dislocative of the anatomy" or the description "my brain being shaken into a sort of mere semi-conscious batter."

Another travelling discomfort was crime ... stick up or bail-up was the description back in Cobb and Co. times. Interestingly today many have a fascination for or even admiration for bushrangers, also called sundowners or highway men ... "Young fellows from the outback farms, the 'wild colonial boys,' with a taste for adventure and no great love of work, and in whose training the moral element had been entirely omitted ... made easy recruits for the old convict bushrangers." Often these fellows received little booty from a bail up, as valuables were sewn in the lining of passengers' clothing, or concealed in the box of one of the wheels, or in the harness. Others had been known to hide their money in the coach curtains, in their hair and even in a carcass of mutton!

Some bail-ups ...

- 1865 Mail stuck up "On Friday last came information of the Condamine and Taroom mail being again stuck up—this time by two men, with their faces covered with sheepskin masks"
- 1870 "a man rushed out of the bush and seizing the bridle of the near side horse cried out to the driver to 'stand' and stop the horses ... the man who endeavoured to stop the coach ... had what appeared to be a dirty handkerchief over his face."
- 1881 "The mailman was on his way down to Dalby from Goondiwindi, met a swagman on the road ... the swagman seized hold of the rein of the pack-horse, drew a six-chambered revolver ... the robber then proceeded to put his own swag on the horse carrying the mail ... mounted the other, and rode away into the bush"

"They were the days when bushrangers flourished, said Mr. Coyle and although I often held the reins of coaches carrying many thousands of pounds' worth of gold—I was only stuck up once. That was at Piper's Flat, and, fortunately, it was at a time when there were neither mails nor gold aboard." Cobb driver Coyle later was appointed to the charge of the North Queensland branch and he went on to say it was not all beer-and-skittles. One of the stages out Hughenden way meant a span of 80 miles without water ... I had charge of 300 men and 2000 horses ... Then the railways came along and as I saw the coaching days were doomed ... I managed to get out at the right time."

Yes, like many things, the era of Cobb and Co. horse coaching, coaching and stores came to an end ... By 1921 "The lights of Cobb and Co. although dimmed, have not yet been extinguished ... nowadays the company has changed from the erratic and risky coaching business to the more stable and lucrative one of storekeeping ... all of the company's mail contracts will terminate on December 31, and they have renewed contracts for only three services, which are of great assistance to the stores in the delivery of goods, inwards and outwards."

Then by 1928 "a fire destroyed the St. George stores and stock, and though business was continued in temporary premises the company has had enough if it ... they have put up a proposal to go into liquidation. That probably will mean the end of Cobb and Company in Queensland—of course except historically—if not in Australia."

In 1929 Two Cobb & Co. Country Stores were for sale "one at Yeulba (stock about £2,000)—and one at Dirranbandi (stock about £5,000)"

However, it was "on August 14, 1924, the last horse-coach trip of the world-renowned firm of Cobb and Co. had been run from Surat to Yeulba ... or to be more precise the Yeulba-St. George coach as it was known for a considerable number of years ... The motor coach has come in its place, but memory of the old conditions will long survive. Who will forget, the coach driver's cheery voice ... 'the elite' sitting up on the box seat ... The arrival and departure ... The coach, with its leather springs and six to eight horses ... portion of the journey was over corduroy ... The coach driver ... the bushman's newspaper ... In most cases the driver would place the mail in the receptacle provided by the selector or station owner ... from a biscuit tin to a zinc-lined box placed about the height from the ground that would allow of the driver placing the letters in it without getting off his seat ... The greatest bugbear to travellers (and my children) was the gate-opening business ; no two gates would be alike, and possibly each had a style of opening patent to itself ... Who will forget the meal served at Lodor's mail change? Roasted goat, prickly pear jam and jelly, splendid home-made bread, to say nothing of the hot scones and 'nanny's' butter, which made up a really 'rich' meal, and that cheered the heart of the traveller for the next stage of the journey." Or of course another of my favourites ... where "the host whipped off the cloth and said to the travellers would you like lamb, ram, mutton or sheep!"

Let's conclude with "The Coach's Story ... Half-hidden in a tangle of tussock and bracken, and bent low to earth as if to hide in shame from curious eyes, it lay — the forlorn relic of what had once been the pride of the road — her Majesty's mail coach ... Two crazy and nearly spokeless wheels alone remained to save it from utter collapse. Shafts, splashboard, seats, windows, fittings, all had disappeared. With its arms folded on the rail of a rickety fence ... What times I have had on the open road; glorious nights when under a full moon the shining quartz track stretched ahead like a silver ribbon, and in the frosty air the sharp ring of eight pairs of shoes made the sparks fly. Drab nights, when thick fog laid a clammy hand on coach and passengers alike ... Days of storm and flood, when my passengers, huddled together in my cosy interior, were startled by a sudden opening of the door ... I served this district faithfully, carrying its people to and fro with comfort and safety ... That was before speed became the god that most travellers worship ... My limbs were now sending forth ominous creaks and groans with the weight of years, and my once handsome coat was sadly the worse for wear. One dreary evening the horses were taken out of the shafts for the last time, and I was dragged to this unused paddock ... among other worn-out servants of man ... Here I am useless and forgotten; yet I had my day — a long one, too — but it has closed. The whisper died away to silence."

To those who first blazed the tracks, groomed the horses, built the change stations, feed the passengers and ensured the delivery of Her Majesty's Mails ... a great debt is due.

Thank you

Reference List - Images

Page 8—ca. 1865 Wattle blossom, South Australia (G. C. Fenton) - Courtesy National Library Australia

Page 10—1869 Sly grog shanty (S. T. Gill 1818-1880) - Courtesy State Library Victoria

Page 13—ca. 1865 Gum blossom, Western Australia (Gertrude Cornelia Fenton 1867-1921) – Courtesy National Library Australia

Page 14—1901 Hill & Co. coach, changing horses (Ernest Gall) - Courtesy State Library of South Australia

Page 15—1912 While the Billy Boils (F. A. Joyner, Adelaide) Supplement to The Australasian Photo-Review, p.213 - Courtesy National Library Australia

Page 16—1950 Flies have dirty feet that carry germs and spread disease : keep homes and yards clean, poster - Courtesy National Library Australia

Page 17—ca. 1850 Bushrangers robbing the mail, Australia (George Lacy 1816-1878?) - Courtesy National Library Australia

Page 18—ca. 1870 The Kelly gang postcard, from an original photograph, Steve Hart, Dan Kelly, Ned Kelly - Courtesy National Library Australia

Page 19—A collection of drawings in watercolour, ink and pencil : illustrative of the life, character & scenery of Melbourne 1850-1862. (William Strutt) - Courtesy State Library New South Wales

Page 20—1857 Street scenes after flood, West Maitland (Elijah Hart) - Courtesy State Library Victoria

Page 21—1860 Sturt's Desert Pea (Charles Norton 1826-1872) - Courtesy State Library Victoria

Page 23—1907 Australia and the bookfellow, Vol. 1 No. 19, 9 May 1907 - Courtesy National Library Australia

Page 24—ca. 1890 His Majesty's Mail wagon in colonial Australia - Courtesy Flickr (by Aussie~mobs, Public Domain Mark)

Page 25—1936 From Cobb's coaches to streamlined cars, 9 May 1935, p.33 – Courtesy National Library Australia

Page 26—1872 Maryland Street Stanthorpe (William Boag) - Courtesy State Library Queensland

Page 27—ca. 1884-1917 A Mail Coach Change (Kerry and Co., Sydney, Australia) –Courtesy Powerhouse Museum

Page 28—1856 Small Choice (Melbourne Punch [Vic. : 1855 - 1900], 3 July, p.2) - Courtesy National Library Australia
"DRAYMAN : I say, mate, which is my best road ? COBB'S DRIVER : I guess that depends on whether you like being smothered in the drink, or jolted to tarnal squash here, best."

Page 29—1906 Woods Point Road, Woods Point (Rev J. Watt) - Courtesy Royal Historical Society of Victoria

Page 30—Horse change, Harold Matthewson's Coach on Stockton-Salt Ash run, Williamtown General Store & blacksmith (Dewhurst) - Courtesy University of Newcastle

Page 31—1880-1930 Mails for Outback (Jim Davidson Australian postcard collection, 1880-1980) – Courtesy National Library Australia

Page 32—1882 In the drought (Published Alfred May and Alfred Martin Ebsworth) - Courtesy State Library Victoria

Page 33—Cabbage Tree Ned (driver) leaving the Black Bull Hotel, Malop Street, Geelong - Courtesy State Library Victoria

Page 34—1817-1818 Blandfordia Nobilis, Album of original drawings (Captain James

Wallis and Joseph Lycett) – Courtesy State Library New South Wales

Page 35—ca. 1854 Coach and horses coming up a hill (Charles Lyall) - Courtesy State Library Victoria

Page 36—1914 The Lone hand, New Series Vol. 1 No. 3 , p.195

Page 37—1867 Flemington racecourse (Thomas Hamilton Lyttleton 1826-1876) - Courtesy State Library Victoria

Page 38—1864 Lantern, Winner of the Melbourne Cup, Derby Stakes and Publican's Purse, wood engraving (Melbourne : Ebenezer and David Syme 1864) - Courtesy State Library Victoria

Page 39—1912 Anthony Horderns Watches and Jewellery, Supplement to The Australasian Photo-Review, p.197 - Courtesy National Library

Page 40—'Cobb & Co. in the [18]fifties,' Pioneering days in western Victoria : a narrative of early station life (James Charles Hamilton 1836-1927)

Page 41—1845 Honeysuckle tree & native dog (Samual Thomas Gill 1818-1880) - Courtesy National Library Australia

Page 42—1870 River Darling opposite Wilcannia, high flood - Courtesy National Library of Australia

Page 43—1842 Purple coral-pea, Botany Bay, N.S. Wales (Harriet Calcott 1804-1866) – Courtesy National Library Australia

Page 44—1890 Adamson's Peak, Port Esperance (J. W. Beattie) - Courtesy National Library Australia

Page 47—ca. 1924 Cobb and Co. coach, Yuleba - Courtesy National Archives Australia

Page 48—1870 Largest kangaroo ever captured : 7 ½ ft . high, seen only in Barnum's Menagerie - Courtesy National Library Australia

Page 50—1932 Cobb's coach at Accallana Well (R. P. Nicholas) - Courtesy State Library South Australia

Page 51—1860 Some of my bush friends in Tasmania : native flowers, berries and insects : drawn from life (Louisa Anne Meredith 1812-1895) – Courtesy National Library Australia

Page 52—ca. 1790 New Holland Creeper, Now known as a New Holland honeyeater, Album of original watercolours of Australian fauna (Sarah Stone) – Courtesy State Library New South Wales

Page 53—View of the coach house and stables at Sedgley Grange, Newmarket (Trackson Family Photograph Albums) - Courtesy State Library of Queensland

Page 54—Banksia praemorsa, Chorizema rhombeum and Patersonia occidentalis (Marrianne Collinson Campbell 1827-1903) – Courtesy National Library Australia

Page 56—Successful Diggers on way from Bendigo (S. T. Gill 1952-1910) - Courtesy State Library Victoria

Page 59—1855 Site of Bently's Hotel, Eureka Ballaarat (James J. Blundell Co. Melbourne 1855) - Courtesy State Library Victoria

Page 60—1856? Monument in the Ballarat cemetery to those who fell at the Eureka Stockade (F. W. Niven) - Courtesy National Library Australia

Page 64—Peacock feather sketch

Page 65—185? Australian Bushmen, view of one mounted man waving to another with his stock whip and hat (E. C. May) - Courtesy State Library New South Wales

Page 66—1910 Cobb & Co. coach arriving in St George, Queensland - Courtesy State Library of Queensland

Page 68—1857 Sheep shearing at a station

near Goulburn (J.R. Clarke) - Courtesy National Library Australia

Page 69—184? Wild dogs devouring sheep (Samuel Thomas Gill 1818-1880) - Courtesy National Library Australia

Page 70—1864 Morgan, the bushranger (Samuel Calvert 1828-1913 engraver) - Courtesy State Library of Victoria

Page 71—1925 Acacia buxifolia (Box-leaved Wattle), Sydney Region - Courtesy National Library Australia

Page 73—1912 Team of horses pulling Cobb & Co coach, Cameron Downs - Courtesy Flinders Shire Historical Collection

Page 74—1850-1888 Album of sketches of St Leonards, Middle Harbour and the Blue Mountains (Rebecca Martens) - Courtesy State Linrary New South Wales

Page 77—1900 Royal mail wagon, Ayr, Queensland - Courtesy State Library Queensland

Page 78—1892 Eucalyptus cordata Labill., family Myrtaceae, 6 March 1892 (R.D. FitzGerald) - Courtesy National Library Australia

Page 79—1904 Motor buggy (Mr Campbell Laird, driver) at Katnook, 9 October 1904 – Courtesy State Library South Australia

Page 80—1880 Five to two bar one : or, "on the road to ruin" (Gibbs, Shallard & Co. printer) - Courtesy State Library Victoria

Page 82—1938 The Old Woolpack Inn, Bacchus Marsh (P. Scott-Williams) – Courtesy State Library Victoria

Page 85—ca. 1909 For The Sake of Auld Lang Syne, postcard - Courtesy Beaconsfield Mine and Hertiage Centre

Page 86—1921 In the Days of Cobb & Co. (Sydney Mail [NSW : 1912 - 1938], 20 April, p.8] - Courtesy State Library New South Wales

Page 87—1826 Acton House, Canberra, built by the First Pioneer, sketch of kangaroos on the back of the postcard (A. J. Bowden) - Courtesy National Museum of Australia

Page 88— ca. 1850 Brickfield Hill, or, High Road to Parramatta (Thomas Watling 1792-?, Rex Nan Kivell Collection) - Courtesy National Library Australia

Page 89—1841-1843 November & Summer & ca. 1870 Royal Arcade, Melbourne (Samuel Thomas Gill (1818-1880) - Courtesy National Library Australia

Page 90—ca. 1850 Gum Wattle (Rex Nan Kivell Collection) - Courtesy National Library Australia

Reference List

1851 'ADJUSTED NEW RUNS.', New South Wales Government Gazette (Sydney, NSW : 1832 - 1900), 12 March, p. 433. , viewed 13 Sep 2024, http://nla.gov.au/nla.news-article230692102

1854 'ADVERTISING', The Argus (Melbourne, Vic.: 1848-1957), 31 Jan, p.3., viewed 20 Jun 2023, http://nla.gov.au/nla.news-article4802637

1856 'AUSTRALIAN DOUBLES.', Melbourne Punch (Vic. : 1855 - 1900), 29 May, p. 6. , viewed 17 Sep 2024, http://nla.gov.au/nla.news-article171431058

1858 'ACCEPTED TENDERS FOR RUNS.', The Moreton Bay Courier (Brisbane, Qld. : 1846 - 1861), 1 May, p. 4. , viewed 13 Sep 2024, http://nla.gov.au/nla.news-article3723396

1859 'TITLE DEEDS.', Mount Alexander Mail (Vic.: 1854-1917), 16 Sep, p.3., viewed 26 Jul 2023, http://nla.gov.au/nla.news-article199046906

1862 'SYDNEY NEWS.', The Maitland Mercury and Hunter River General Advertiser (NSW : 1843 - 1893), 3 July, p. 3. , viewed 06 Jun 2023, http://nla.gov.au/nla.news-article18689254

1863 'MORUYA REGATTA.', Empire (Sydney, NSW : 1850 - 1875), 3 February, p. 2. , viewed 20 Sep 2024, http://nla.gov.au/nla.news-article60522296

1865 'ADELAIDE.', The Sydney Morning Herald (NSW : 1842 - 1954), 1 December, p. 5. , viewed 20 Sep 2024, http://nla.gov.au/nla.news-article13122551

1865 'CLASSIFIED ADVERTISING', The Brisbane Courier (Qld. : 1864 - 1933), 29 December, p. 1. , viewed 17 Dec 2024, http://nla.gov.au/nla.news-article1284772

1866 'GOVERNMENT LAND SALES.', The Brisbane Courier (Qld. : 1864 - 1933), 1 February, p. 2. , viewed 13 Sep 2024, http://nla.gov.au/nla.news-article1261697

1866 'MAIL PUNCTUALITY.', The Brisbane Courier (Qld. : 1864 - 1933), 2 March, p. 3. , viewed 09 Dec 2024, http://nla.gov.au/nla.news-article1263461

1867 'ADVERTISING', Dalby Herald and Western Queensland Advertiser (Qld. : 1866 - 1879), 2 February, p. 1. , viewed 13 Sep 2024, http://nla.gov.au/nla.news-article215453113

1867 'BATHURST.', Sydney Mail (NSW : 1860 - 1871), 6 July, p. 4. , viewed 20 Sep 2024, http://nla.gov.au/nla.news-article166798754

1868 'TERRIBLE SUFFERING.', The Newcastle Chronicle (NSW : 1866 - 1876), 23 May, p. 1. (Supplement to the Newcastle Chronicle), viewed 22 Sep 2024, http://nla.gov.au/nla.news-article111331605

1872 'POETRY, ORIGINAL AND SELECTED.', South Australian Register (Adelaide, SA : 1839 - 1900), 22 January, p. 7. , viewed 20 Sep 2024, http://nla.gov.au/nla.news-article39264664

1872 'STANTHORPE.', Dalby Herald and Western Queensland Advertiser (Qld. : 1866 - 1879), 24 August, p. 2. , viewed 27 Sep 2024, http://nla.gov.au/nla.news-article215602654

1875 'COBB & CO.' Gympie Times and Mary River Mining Gazette (Qld. : 1868 - 1919), 5 May, p. 4. , viewed 19 Sep 2024, http://nla.gov.au/nla.news-article168911735

1875 'COBB'S BOX.', Wagga Wagga Advertiser and Riverine Reporter (NSW : 1868 - 1875), 6 February, p. 4. , viewed 19 Sep 2024, http://nla.gov.au/nla.news-article104117694

1876 'PAUL PRY'S TRIP ON THE WESTERN ROAD.', Western Star and Roma Advertiser (Qld. : 1875 - 1948), 12 August, p. 3. , viewed 13 Sep 2024, http://nla.gov.au/nla.news-article97421161

1876 'SURAT.', The Week (Brisbane, Qld. : 1876 - 1934), 8 April, p. 9. , viewed 13 Sep 2024, http://nla.gov.au/nla.news-article184998656

1877 'NEWS OF THE DAY.', The Herald (Melbourne, Vic. : 1861 - 1954), 21 June, p. 2. , viewed 22 Sep 2024, http://nla.gov.au/nla.news-article244265521

1878 'DEATH OF THE FOUNDER OF COBB AND CO.', The Goulburn Herald and Chronicle (NSW : 1864 - 1881), 28 September, p. 3. , viewed 21 Nov 2024, http://nla.gov.au/nla.news-article100879416

1878 'MARYBOROUGH.', The Queenslander (Brisbane, Qld. : 1866 - 1939), 28 December, p. 391. , viewed 20 Sep 2024, http://nla.gov.au/nla.news-article19778161

1878 'SURAT.', The Queenslander (Brisbane, Qld. : 1866 - 1939), 2 February, p. 7. , viewed 13 Sep 2024, http://nla.gov.au/nla.news-article19764474

1879 'ADVERTISING', The Telegraph (Brisbane, Qld. : 1872 - 1947), 17 June, p. 3. , viewed 13 Sep 2024, http://nla.gov.au/nla.news-article169503531

1879 'ADVERTISING', Western Star and Roma Advertiser (Qld. : 1875 - 1948), 15 March, p. 2. , viewed 13 Sep 2024, http://nla.gov.au/nla.news-article97448620

1879 'ADVERTISING', Western Star and Roma Advertiser (Qld. : 1875 - 1948), 20 October, p. 4. , viewed 13 Sep 2024, http://nla.gov.au/nla.news-article97449683

1879 'CLASSIFIED ADVERTISING', The Brisbane Courier (Qld. : 1864 - 1933), 17 June, p. 1. , viewed 13 Sep 2024, http://nla.gov.au/nla.news-article888265

1879 'GENERAL EPITOME.', The Week (Brisbane, Qld. : 1876 - 1934), 12 April, p. 15. , viewed 13 Sep 2024, http://nla.gov.au/nla.news-article181838440

1879 'ORIGINAL CORRESPONDENCE.', Western Star and Roma Advertiser (Qld. : 1875 - 1948), 14 July, p. 3. , viewed 13 Sep 2024, http://nla.gov.au/nla.news-article97449213

1879 'ORIGINAL CORRESPONDENCE.', Western Star and Roma Advertiser (Qld. : 1875 - 1948), 7 July, p. 3. , viewed 13 Sep 2024, http://nla.gov.au/nla.news-article97449174

1879 'OUR BRISBANE LETTER.', The Sydney Morning Herald (NSW : 1842 - 1954), 31 October, p. 7. , viewed 13 Sep 2024, http://nla.gov.au/nla.news-article13441586

1880 'A BUSH TRIP.', Australian Town and Country Journal (Sydney, NSW : 1870 - 1919), 3 January, p. 18. , viewed 20 Sep 2024, http://nla.gov.au/nla.news-article70939913

1880 'ACTION FOR DAMAGES.', Western Star and Roma Advertiser (Qld. : 1875 - 1948), 26 June, p. 3. , viewed 13 Sep 2024, http://nla.gov.au/nla.news-article97451001

1880-1889 'NIVEN'S GUIDE BOOK AND SOUVENIR OF BALLARAT : THE GARDEN CITY OF VICTORIA', F. W. Niven, https://trove.nla.gov.au/9?keyword=%27History%20of%20Ballarat%27%20by%20Withers

1886 'BUNGIL DIVISIONAL BOARD.', Western Star and Roma Advertiser (Qld. : 1875 - 1948), 8 December, p. 2. , viewed 30 Sep 2024, http://nla.gov.au/nla.news-article102551466

1886 'ORIGINAL TALE.', The Capricornian (Rockhampton, Qld. : 1875 - 1929), 18 December, p. 9. (Christmas Supplement), viewed 27 Sep 2024, http://nla.gov.au/nla.news-article66318305

1886 'SUMMARY FOR EUROPE.', The Brisbane Courier (Qld. : 1864 - 1933), 24 February, p. 3. , viewed 13 Sep 2024, http://nla.gov.au/nla.news-article4493235

1886 'TO MR PAT GOOLEY, OF MESSRS COBB AND CO.', The Yarrawonga Mercury and Mulwala (N.S.W.) News (Vic. : 1882 - 1892; 1894 - 1897), 13 May, p. 3. , viewed 18 Sep 2024, http://nla.gov.au/nla.news-article273512708

1887 'AULD LANG SYNE.', Nepean Times (Penrith, NSW : 1882 - 1962), 8 October, p. 2. , viewed 18 Dec 2024, http://nla.gov.au/nla.news-article100896858

1887 'THE FAMILY DOCTOR.', The Herald (Melbourne, Vic. : 1861 - 1954), 24 December, p. 3. , viewed 09 Dec 2024, http://nla.gov.au/nla.news-article241430937

1887 'BALL'S HEAD.', The Sydney Morning Herald (NSW : 1842 - 1954), 26 October, p. 7. , viewed 22 Sep 2024, http://nla.gov.au/nla.news-article13669003

1888 'SNAKE BITE.', Kerang Times and Swan Hill Gazette (Vic. : 1877 - 1889), 13 January, p. 5. , viewed 17 Dec 2024, http://nla.gov.au/nla.news-article65610394

1889 The Palace Hotel (Bourke Street) guide to Melbourne. Manufacturer (Melbourne : Fergusson & Mitchell) httpe://viewer.slv.vic.gov.y=IE4357277&file=FL18598840&mode=browser

1900 'THE ROARING DAYS.', The Worker (Wagga, NSW : 1892 - 1913), 15 September, p. 7. , viewed 19 Jan 2025, http://nla.gov.au/nla.news-article145899086

1891 'A SNAKE YARN.', Windsor and Richmond Gazette (NSW : 1888 - 1971), 12 September, p. 10. , viewed 20 Sep 2024, http://nla.gov.au/nla.news-article72540894

1892 'AULD LANG SYNE.', The Pictorial Australian (Adelaide, SA : 1885 - 1895), 1 October, p. 13. , viewed 18 Dec 2024, http://nla.gov.au/nla.news-article230506880

1893 'A STREET RUNAWAY.', Geelong Advertiser (Vic. : 1859 - 1929), 9 September, p. 3. , viewed 17 Dec 2024, http://nla.gov.au/nla.news-article150747819

1893 'CASTLEMAINE.', Leader (Melbourne, Vic. : 1862 - 1918, 1935), 30 September, p. 31. , viewed 21 Nov 2024, http://nla.gov.au/nla.news-article196642404

1893 'COBB AND COMPANY.', The Australian Star (Sydney, NSW : 1887 - 1909), 22 March, p. 6. , viewed 15 Aug 2023, http://nla.gov.au/nla.newsarticle227167669

1895 'COBB AND CO.', Warwick Argus (Qld. : 1879 - 1901), 30 March, p. 4. , viewed 17 Sep 2024, http://nla.gov.au/nla.news-article76649248

1896 'THE BUSHRANGER.', Australian Town and Country Journal (Sydney, NSW : 1870 - 1919), 8 February, p. 10. , viewed 22 Nov 2024, http://nla.gov.au/nla.news-article71241687

1897 'CHRISTMAS HOLIDAYS.', The Norseman Pioneer (WA : 1896 - 1897), 11 December, p. 3. , viewed 17 Dec 2024, http://nla.gov.au/nla.news-article163904175

1897 'CHRISTMAS NUMBER OF THE BULLETIN' Vol. 18 No. 930 (11 Dec 1897), Created/Published Sydney, N.S.W.: John Haynes and J.F. Archibald, 1880-1984. https://nla.gov.au/nla.obj-691854470/view?sectionId=nla.obj-721915524&searchTerm=1897+%22Such+-days+as+when+the+Royal+Mail+was+run+by+Cobb+and+Co.%22&partId=nla.obj-691865821#page/n8/mode/1up)

1897 'ORIGINAL POETRY.', The Australasian (Melbourne, Vic. : 1864 - 1946), 2 January, p. 42. , viewed 18 Sep 2024, http://nla.gov.au/nla.news-article139735739

1898 'REMINISCENCES OF COBB AND CO.', The Riverine Grazier (Hay, NSW: 1873-1954), 14 Jan, p.2., viewed 31

May 2023, http://nla.gov.au/nla.news-article140688564

1900 'A DROWNING ACCIDENT.', The Western Champion and General Advertiser for the Central-Western Districts (Barcaldine, Qld. : 1892 - 1922), 27 November, p. 9. , viewed 17 Dec 2024, http://nla.gov.au/nla.news-article76564358

1900 'THE ROARING DAYS.', The Worker (Wagga, NSW : 1892 - 1913), 15 September, p. 7. , viewed 17 Sep 2024, http://nla.gov.au/nla.news-article145899086

1900 'THE POET'S CORNER', The Western Champion and General Advertiser for the Central-Western Districts (Barcaldine, Qld. : 1892 - 1922), 20 November, p. 10. , viewed 18 Sep 2024, http://nla.gov.au/nla.news-article76564309

1901 'ORIGINAL POETRY.', The Australasian (Melbourne, Vic. : 1864 - 1946), 21 September, p. 50. , viewed 20 Sep 2024, http://nla.gov.au/nla.news-article139746813

1901 'THE WOMEN OF THE WEST.', The Charleville Times (Brisbane, Qld. : 1896 - 1954), 2 November, p. 4. , viewed 30 Sep 2024, http://nla.gov.au/nla.news-article76672996

1902 'A BALLAD FOR COBB AND CO.', Table Talk (Melbourne, Vic. : 1885 - 1939), 15 May, p. 15. , viewed 17 Sep 2024, http://nla.gov.au/nla.news-article145706871

1902 'MY LIFE IN MANY STATES AND IN FOREIGN LANDS.', Train, George Francis. Pp. Xxi. 340. D. Appleton: New York. SR 910.4 T768. Available from: The National Library of Australia

1903 'COBB AND CO.', Windsor and Richmond Gazette (NSW : 1888 - 1971), 10 January, p. 1. , viewed 15 Sep 2024, http://nla.gov.au/nla.news-article86217886

1904 'THE DAYS OF COBB AND CO.' The Campbelltown Herald (NSW : 1880 - 1919) 5 October 1904: 3. Web. 18 Sep 2024 <http://nla.gov.au/nla.news-article102480508>.

1905 'PERSONAL PARS.', Molong Argus (NSW : 1896 - 1921), 14 April, p. 8. , viewed 19 Sep 2024, http://nla.gov.au/nla.news-article144363560

1906 'THE RATTLE OF THE COACH.', The Sydney Mail and New South Wales Advertiser (NSW : 1871 - 1912), 26 December, p. 1650. , viewed 17 Sep 2024, http://nla.gov.au/nla.news-article163683489

1908 'ORIGINAL POETRY.', The Australasian (Melbourne, Vic. : 1864 - 1946), 25 January, p. 51. , viewed 16 Sep 2024, http://nla.gov.au/nla.news-article139208276

1908 'THE CONTRIBUTOR', The Sydney Mail and New South Wales Advertiser (NSW : 1871 - 1912), 25 November, p. 1405. , viewed 21 Nov 2024, http://nla.gov.au/nla.news-article163229756

1908 'THE DAY OF COBB AND CO.', Windsor and Richmond Gazette (NSW : 1888 - 1971), 19 December, p. 12. , viewed 19 Sep 2024, http://nla.gov.au/nla.news-article85868172

1911 'A PIONEER OF THE COACHING DAYS: THE LATE JAMES RUTHERFORD.', The Sydney Mail and New South Wales Advertiser (NSW : 1871 - 1912), 20 September, p. 26. , viewed 14 Sep 2023, http://nla.gov.au/nla.news-article164334352

1911 'BUSHRANGER TRICKED.', Tungamah and Lake Rowan Express and St. James Gazette (Vic. : 1883 - 1920), 9 March, p. 6. , viewed 20 Sep 2024, http://nla.gov.au/nla.news-article270141053

1912 'A FUNNY STORY.', Chronicle (Adelaide, SA: 1895-1954), 8 Jun, p.21., viewed 11 Apr 2024, http://nla.gov.au/nla.newsarticle88699036

1919 'THE COACH DRIVER', The Australian Worker (Sydney, NSW : 1913 - 1950), 26 June, p. 13. , viewed 17 Sep 2024, http://nla.gov.au/nla.news-article145775020

1919 'IN THE WEST.', Toowoomba Chronicle (Qld. : 1902 - 1922), 29 August, p. 6. , viewed 28 Oct 2024, http://nla.gov.au/nla.news-article253023687

1919 'VERSE.', The Wingham Chronicle and Manning River Observer (NSW : 1898 - 1954), 7 March, p. 4. , viewed 19 Jan 2025, http://nla.gov.au/nla.news-article166905691

1920 'ON THE ROADS WITH COBB & CO.', Smith's Weekly (Sydney, NSW : 1919 - 1950), 4 September, p. 9. , viewed 20 Sep 2024, http://nla.gov.au/nla.news-article234221223

1922 'OLD COACHING DAYS.', The Argus (Melbourne, Vic.: 1848-1957), 10 Jun, p.7., viewed 06 Aug 2021, http://nla.gov.au/nla

1922 'MEMORIES.', The Northern Miner (Charters Towers, Qld. : 1874 - 1954), 14 July, p. 6. , viewed 16 Sep 2024, http://nla.gov.au/nla.news-article80523454

1922 'THE PIONEERS.', West Gippsland Gazette (Warragul, Vic.: 1898 - 1930), 28 Feb, p.3. (MORNING.), viewed 02 May 2024, http://nla.gov.au/nla.news-article68625607

1924 'GOOD-BYE TO COBB & CO.', The Cessnock Eagle and South Maitland Recorder (NSW : 1913 - 1954), 5 September, p. 4. , viewed 17 Sep 2024, http://nla.gov.au/nla.news-article99376376

1924 'LOCAL AND GENERAL', Daily Examiner (Grafton, NSW : 1915 - 1954), 31 December, p. 4. , viewed 17 Dec 2024, http://nla.gov.au/nla.news-article195794745

1924 'THE FOUNDER OF COBB & CO.', The Scone Advocate (NSW : 1887 - 1954), 12 December, p. 4. , viewed 09 Dec 2024, http://nla.gov.au/nla.news-article157136209

1924 'THE LAST COACH.', Balonne Beacon (St. George,

Qld. : 1909 - 1954), 30 August, p. 3. , viewed 16 Sep 2024, http://nla.gov.au/nla.news-article218940070

1924 'THE LAST COACH', The Week (Brisbane, Qld.: 1876-1934), 5 Sep, p.16., viewed 09 Apr 2024, http://nla.gov.au/nla.news-article187198700

1924 'THE DAYS OF COBB & CO.', Macleay Argus (Kempsey, NSW : 1885 - 1907; 1909 - 1910; 1912 - 1913; 1915 - 1916; 1918 - 1954), 8 February, p. 3. , viewed 18 Sep 2024, http://nla.gov.au/nla.news-article234452157

1924 'THE FOUNDER OF COBB & CO.', The Scone Advocate (NSW : 1887 - 1954), 12 December, p. 4. , viewed 08 Jun 2023, http://nla.gov.au/nla.news-article157136209

1924 'TOPICAL TALK', The Australian Worker (Sydney, NSW : 1913 - 1950), 27 August, p. 10. , viewed 16 Sep 2024, http://nla.gov.au/nla.news-article145948293

1925 'Coaching in the Commonwealth', Sunday Times (Perth, WA : 1902 - 1954), 7 June, p. 11. , viewed 20 Sep 2024, http://nla.gov.au/nla.news-article58219105

1925 'COBB'S COACHES.', The Brisbane Courier (Qld. : 1864 - 1933), 17 January, p. 17. , viewed 18 Sep 2024, http://nla.gov.au/nla.news-article20898443

1925 'SHADOW OF COBB & CO.', The Voice of the North (NSW : 1918 - 1933), 10 September, p. 18. , viewed 18 Sep 2024, http://nla.gov.au/nla.news-article112244413

1926 'FAREWELL TO W. ROCHESTER', The Wingham Chronicle and Manning River Observer (NSW : 1898 - 1954) 31 August 1926: 4. Web. 13 Sep 2024 http://nla.gov.au/nla.news-article166284568

1926 'FAREWELL TO MR. W. ROCHESTER', The Northern Champion (Taree, NSW : 1913 - 1954), 28 August, p. 6. , viewed 18 Sep 2024, http://nla.gov.au/nla.news-article161595001

1928 'THOSE WERE THE DAYS!', The Herald (Melbourne, Vic. : 1861 - 1954), 8 May, p. 6. , viewed 22 Sep 2024, http://nla.gov.au/nla.news-article243987674

1930 'COBB & CO.'S OLDEST DRIVER.', The Propeller (Hurstville, NSW : 1911 - 1954), 13 June, p. 3. , viewed 09 Dec 2024, http://nla.gov.au/nla.news-article235050032

1931 'EARLY DAYS.', Narromine News and Trangie Advocate (NSW : 1898 - 1955), 24 July, p. 7. , viewed 20 Sep 2024, http://nla.gov.au/nla.news-article98921371

1931 'IN THE DAYS OF COBB AND CO.', Northern Star (Lismore, NSW : 1876 - 1954), 18 November, p. 4. , viewed 18 Sep 2024, http://nla.gov.au/nla.news-article94258607

1932 'AUSTRALIANITIES', Glen Innes Examiner (NSW : 1908 - 1954), 3 September, p. 2. , viewed 22 Sep 2024, http://nla.gov.au/nla.news-article184608041

1932 'WHIPS OF COBB AND CO.', Sydney Mail (NSW : 1912 - 1938), 24 February, p. 15. , viewed 22 Sep 2024, http://nla.gov.au/nla.news-article160082745

1934 'COACHING AND THE COACHING DAYS.', The Riverine Grazier (Hay, NSW : 1873 - 1954), 13 February, p. 4. , viewed 17 Sep 2024, http://nla.gov.au/nla.news-article136892195

1934 'THE COACH'S STORY.', The Age (Melbourne, Vic. : 1854 - 1954), 2 June, p. 4. , viewed 30 Sep 2024, http://nla.gov.au/nla.news-article204825626

1935 'VETERAN COACH AND COACHMAN', The Argus (Melbourne, Vic. : 1848 - 1957), 8 June, p. 24. , viewed 17 Dec 2024, http://nla.gov.au/nla.news-article12246865

1935 'Yeulba', The Queenslander Illustrated Weekly (Brisbane, Qld. : 1927 - 1939), 2 May, p. 2. , viewed 13 Sep 2024, http://nla.gov.au/nla.news-article27507684

1937 'A [?] DRIVE', The Australasian (Melbourne, Vic.: 1864-1946), 31 Jul, p.7., viewed 12 Oct 2022, http://nla.gov.au/nla.newsarticle141807670

1937 'GOLD-DIGGING DAYS', Lithgow Mercury (NSW : 1898 - 1954), 18 June, P. 8. (Town Edition), viewed 20 Sep 2024, http://nla.gov.au/nla.news-article221865361

1937 'NEWS OF THE DAY.', The Age (Melbourne, Vic. : 1854 - 1954), 25 May, p. 10. , viewed 20 Sep 2024, http://nla.gov.au/nla.news-article203877840

1937 'OLD TIMES', The Inverell Times (NSW : 1899 - 1907, 1909 - 1954), 29 September, p. 8. , viewed 09 Dec 2024, http://nla.gov.au/nla.news-article185379499

1937 'ONE SECRET OF OLD AGE.', Newcastle Morning Herald and Miners' Advocate (NSW : 1876 - 1954), 28 May, p. 12. , viewed 19 Jan 2025, http://nla.gov.au/nla.news-article133545074

1938 COACH POSTER, State Library Victoria

1938 'ON THE TRACK.', Townsville Daily Bulletin (Qld. : 1907 - 1954), 31 August, p. 11. , viewed 20 Sep 2024, http://nla.gov.au/nla.news-article62166056

1938 'THE QUEENSLAND PLACE NAMES COMMITTEE.', The Cairns Post (Qld. : 1909 - 1954), 5 July, p. 9. , viewed 13 Sep 2024, http://nla.gov.au/nla.news-article42129122

1939 'COBB AND CO.', The World's News (Sydney, NSW : 1901 - 1955), 29 July, p. 45. , viewed 13 Sep 2024, http://nla.gov.au/nla.news-article131492264

1939 'THE COACH DRIVERS', The Bulletin, Created/Published Sydney, N.S.W.: John Haynes and J.F. Archibald, 1880-1984 7 Jun 1939, p.20 https://nla.gov.au/nla.obj-578436455/view?sectionId=nla.obj-583239899&searchTerm=%22The

+whip+cracks+echoed+the+pistol+shot%22&partId=nla.obj-578457311#page/n0/mode/1up

1940-1941 'COBB & CO.'S OLD COACH DRIVERS' ASSOCIATION'. Annual report. [Footscray, The Association]. State Library Victoria.

1941 'EUREKA STOCKADE', Labor Call (Melbourne, Vic. : 1906 - 1953), 3 April, p. 1. , viewed 18 Sep 2024, http://nla.gov.au/nla.news-article249645148

1941 'THE DAY BEFORE YESTERDAY', Western Mail (Perth, WA : 1885 - 1954), 18 December, p. 41. , viewed 27 Sep 2024, http://nla.gov.au/nla.news-article37949012

1942 ANNUAL REPORT / COBB & CO.'S OLD COACH DRIVERS' ASSOCIATION, 1942, pp.6&7. State Library Victoria.

1942 'MELBOURNE CUP', Smith's Weekly (Sydney, NSW : 1919 - 1950), 21 November, p. 20. , viewed 27 Sep 2024, http://nla.gov.au/nla.news-article234588577

1945 'CLAPP: RAILWAYMAN WIT [?]H A ONE-TRACK MIND', The Daily Telegraph (Sydney, NSW : 1931 - 1954), 25 August, p. 10. , viewed 21 Nov 2024, http://nla.gov.au/nla.news-article247639769

1947 'CONTRIBUTIONS FROM MEMBERS TRY YOUR HAND AT ORIGINAL SKETCHES SEND IN ORIGINAL STORIES POEMS AND PUZZLES', The Sydney Morning Herald (NSW : 1842 - 1954), 16 April, p. 10. (Playtime Children's Newspaper), viewed 20 Sep 2024, http://nla.gov.au/nla.news-article18021529

1950 'REMINISCENCES OF COACHING DAYS', Morning Bulletin (Rockhampton, Qld. : 1878 - 1954), 23 March, pp. 8&9. , viewed 20 Sep 2024, http://nla.gov.au/nla.news-article56937460

1851 'ADJUSTED NEW RUNS.', New South Wales Government Gazette (Sydney, NSW : 1832 - 1900), 12 March, p. 433. , viewed 19 Jan 2025, http://nla.gov.au/nla.news-article230692102

1951 'IN THE DAYS OF COBB & CO.', Narromine News and Trangie Advocate (NSW : 1898 - 1955), 19 January, p. 2. , viewed 27 Sep 2024, http://nla.gov.au/nla.news-article100191539

1951 'THE DAYS OF COBB AND CO.', The World's News (Sydney, NSW : 1901 - 1955), 21 July, p. 12. , viewed 27 Sep 2024, http://nla.gov.au/nla.news-article139911061

1951 'SHE DROVE FOR COBB AND CO.', Weekly Times (Melbourne, Vic. : 1869 - 1954), 22 August, p. 32. , viewed 02 Oct 2024, http://nla.gov.au/nla.news-article224486334

1952 'WOMAN'S STORY OF HARD LIFE ON MAIL CHANGE', Barrier Miner (Broken Hill, NSW : 1888 - 1954), 25 September, p. 8. , viewed 22 Sep 2024, http://nla.gov.au/nla.news-article61219214

1953 'DEATH OF MR. S.C. COLEMAN', Western Herald (Bourke, NSW : 1887 - 1970), 16 January, p. 6. , viewed 22 Sep 2024, http://nla.gov.au/nla.news-article103924864

1863 'MORUYA REGATTA.', Empire (Sydney, NSW : 1850 - 1875), 3 February, p. 2. , viewed 19 Jan 2025, http://nla.gov.au/nla.news-article60522296

2024 GLOSSARY OF POETIC TERMS, POETRY FOUNDATION https://www.poetryfoundation.org/education/glossary/

www.ingramcontent.com/pod-product-compliance
Lightning Source LLC
Chambersburg PA
CBHW041711290426
44109CB00028B/2844